SUBJUGATED
VOLUME I

◆

Research

SUBJUGATED

VOLUME I

Research

"A More Likely Explanation"

THE REVELATION

Apparently, we wandered the earth for 100,000 years and then suddenly began building cities around 2,200 B.C.

Who are we? ... Really!

By taking ancient writing at face value, we find "dull" Human primates upgraded around 4,000 B.C. to become Homo Sapiens. But how, and why?

What happened, before and after the flood?

What genetic traits still stand buried in us from those times?

Are we a balanced, natural species, or are we unbalanced and conflicted both amongst ourselves and with our environment?

Why do today's left and right not fathom the thoughts of the other?

Sumerian, Hebrew, Egyptian, Greek, Indus Valley, Yellow River, Mayan and American Indian voices still speak through their writings.

Shouldn't we be listening?

Drawing from the earliest accounts of humankind, *Subjugated,* by historian *Joe Patrina,* suggests the true origins of Homo Sapiens as voiced by ancient writers who actually witnessed Homo Sapient subjugation by their Alien overlords.

By becoming clear eyed as to how outsiders transitioned simple Human primates into advanced Homo Sapiens, we next learn how this experiment played out once Homo Sapiens strove for freedom.

From 200,000 to 4,000 B.C., primitive humans wandered, a primate species that never progressed, troop based, chief dominated, with no tolerance for individuals – dependent upon nature.

In 4,000 B.C., Aliens arrive looking to exploit resources, at heart adventurers, espousing self-reliance, risk taking, social mobility and technology - masters of nature.

Genetically, the two mix to make "us", the Homo Sapiens, a new breed of teachable workers.

But the hybrid human runs volatile, prone to emotional imbalance, violence, acting aggressively against nature, and perpetually conflicted by unreconcilable primate and alien traits.

God and evolution have nothing to do with it.

Ever since, genetic conflict plays out, a battle between primate cravings for managed societies and alien impulses for liberty.

What are we to do with ourselves?

HUMANITY UNRAVELED

In Three (3) Volumes

After years of digging for insights buried within historical texts, many urged me to summarize the findings into "a more likely explanation" of humankind's origins. Findings are organized across three (3) volumes.

VOLUME I
RESEARCH

"A More Likely Explanation"

... offering fresh views of ancient writings, seeing them as "sincere accounts" of what Homo Sapiens actually witnessed during the 4,000 B.C. to A.D.1,000 expanse of the early Homo Sapient race.

VOLUME II
The PRIMATES & ALIENS Series

"History Re-imagined"

... a five-season, 35 episode series that retro-fits the formative years of the Homo Sapient species within the primate/alien context – covering Sumerian, Hebrew, Egyptian, Indian, Chinese, Greek and American episodes.

VOLUME III
GENETICS DRIVES POLITICAL PREFERENCE

"Primate/Alien Conflict Now"

... applies the theory that one's genetic pull is either more Primate or more Alien, and that *this pull alone* determines one's political preference for socialism versus libertarianism, logic superfluous.

Copyright © 2022 by J.A. Patrina.

All rights reserved. No part of this book may be reproduced in any form or by any electronic or mechanical means, including information storage and retrieval systems, without permission in writing from the publisher, except by reviewers, who may quote brief passages in a review.

This publication contains the opinions and ideas of its author. It is intended to provide helpful and informative material on the subjects addressed in the publication. The authors and publisher specifically disclaim all responsibility for any liability, loss, or risk, personal or otherwise, which is incurred as a consequence, directly or indirectly, of the use and application of any of the contents of this book.

ISBN: 978-1-7330672-4-9   [Paperback Edition]

Printed and bound in The United States of America.

Published by LittleHouse Enterprises Inc.

JOE PATRINA is a singer/songwriter, researcher, book author and technology entrepreneur. Please visit: *JoePatrina.com*

"A MORE LIKELY EXPLANATION"

Proof of historical events becomes daunting the further back in time one goes. The early Homo Sapient writings that are relied upon here in *Subjugated* – Sumerian, Hebrew, Indian, Chinese, Greek, Mayan, Cherokee writings, etc. - have the additional problem of ancient writers being limited by the knowledge shortcomings of their era, easily misinterpreting what they saw.

Nevertheless, the words of the ancients represent sincere accounts of the past which we can then upgrade by applying today's improved level of scientific and historical awareness. This upgrade process yields a still imperfect, yet "more likely explanation" of Homo Sapient origins than do prior interpretations.

BEFORE WE GET STARTED ...

Please consider these:

In the end, more than freedom, they wanted security. They wanted a comfortable life, and they lost it all—security, comfort, and freedom. When the Athenians finally wanted not to give to society but for society to give to them, when the freedom they wished for most was freedom from responsibility, then Athens ceased to be free and was never free again. — **Edward Gibbon**

The policy of American government is to leave its citizens free, neither restraining them nor aiding them in their pursuits. - **Thomas Jefferson**

The founders of the United States based their design upon the following: Our libertarian rights to life, liberty and property sit above any operation of government; laws cannot be enacted that do away with these inalienable rights. — **J. A. Patrina**

It is true that liberty is precious; so precious that it must be carefully rationed. — **Vladimir Lenin**

* * *

Democracy is indispensable to socialism. — **Vladimir Lenin**

* * *

Democracy passes into despotism. — **Plato**

* * *

Only Americans can hurt America. — **Dwight D. Eisenhower**

About the time of the end, a body of men will be raised up who will turn their attention to the Prophecies, and in the midst of much clamor and opposition insist upon their literal interpretation. —**Sir Isaac Newton**

* * *

When I am traveling in a carriage, or walking after a good meal, or during the night when I cannot sleep; it is on such occasions that ideas flow best and most abundantly. —**Wolfgang Amadeus Mozart**

* * *

I think and think for months and years. Ninety-nine times, the conclusion is false. The hundredth time I am right. —**Albert Einstein**

* * *

I know this world is ruled by infinite intelligence. —**Thomas Edison**

* * *

The eyes of that species of extinct Giants, whose bones fill the mounds of America, have gazed on Niagara, as ours do now. —**Abraham Lincoln**

* * *

The intellect has little to do with the road to discovery. There comes a leap in consciousness, call it intuition or what you will, and the solution comes to you, and you don't know how or why. —**Albert Einstein**

All of these assorted statements are explained herein.

CONTENTS

Author's Note		xiv
Preface:		xvii
CHAPTER 1:	Intervention, the Alternative History	1
CHAPTER 2:	Homo Sapiens, How Old Are We?	10
CHAPTER 3:	Prove It! History Requires Imagination	17
CHAPTER 4:	Moses & "the Lord"… Partners	20
CHAPTER 5:	Genetics, Accounting for Sudden Change	31
CHAPTER 6:	Enoch & The Book of Enoch, The Watchers	45
CHAPTER 7:	Moses Moves East, The Assault	50
CHAPTER 8:	Time & the Speed of Physics: How Much Gets Done Per Second	57
CHAPTER 9:	Noah's Ark, The Flood, Babel & The Diaspora	67
CHAPTER 10:	Language, before 1,000 BC, A Slow Start	79
CHAPTER 11:	Joshua, 1400 B.C., The Extermination of Nephilim in Canaan	91
CHAPTER 12	Evidence From Other Civilizations	97
CHAPTER 13:	Renegade Primate/Aliens The Bigfoot Species	111
CHAPTER 14:	Renegade Primate/Aliens The Little People	115
CHAPTER 15:	Renegade Primate/Aliens The Ohio Giants	123
CHAPTER 16:	Collusion—History Suppressed, Primate Control Over Narratives	128
CHAPTER 17:	Plato & the World of Ideas	132
Epilogue		145

SUBJUGATED

VOLUME I – RESEARCH, CONTEMPLATION & REVELATION

Author's Note

This book suggests that everything we have heard about ourselves happened "just recently," and more so, that it all happened much differently than told. Get ready to be open minded. In this "Author's Note" segment I will lay out the key findings. Please don't panic!

What really happened?

The "than-told" version has it that primates slowly evolved into modern-day humans about 200,000 years ago, eventually leaving East Africa to wander the globe for 70,000 years, only to achieve a few stone tools, cave paintings, fire, camp dogs and some pottery, until ... "out of the blue," humans began to create and congregate in cities around 2,200 BC.

Moreover, the traditional narrative claims that every Homo Sapient advance started and ended in isolation here on Earth; neither God nor Aliens applied any influence. Apparently, in seclusion, we suddenly blossomed, and supposedly, we continue to evolve today—no questions, please. That's the science-community's party-line, especially the "no questions" part.

The historical chapters of SUBJUGATED contend that around 4,000 BC, the mentioned hunter/gatherer humanoid species was "upgraded" in vitro (via test tube) with *select* Alien DNA strands implanted into fertilized human eggs. This resulted in *us*, the *Homo Sapiens*, effectively the manufactured, intelligent, trainable livestock of Alien overlords. Again, please don't panic... at least not yet! I will provide much to support this.

Besides gaining higher intellect, the new Homo Sapiens emerged conflicted, as traits from the Primates and the Aliens did not sit right with each other, as follows:

> Primate Humans emerged from a communal way of life, with a chief ape ruling over his troop, his subordinates all sharing second-tier status. This subservient trait, still present in Homo Sapiens, underpins today's socialist political model. But now, in our upgraded form, a single strong ape no longer dominates over the others. The modern socialist system operates scalable, employing a pyramid of command sitting above common citizens – think China - managed by a hierarchy of elite dominate ape confederates. Still, as in the past, no rebellion tolerated.

> Aliens came from an opposite existence, living lives of adventure and exploration, characterized by risk-taking and independent thinking, a tad rebellious. This life of quest and entrepreneurial spirit transitioned into today's libertarian political model, where each pursues their own path. The Alien side, though, being hyper-individualistic, is not as "smooth sailing" as, say, U.S. Navy officers. Historic references show that rivalries, fiefdoms, and warfare existed amongst these liberty lovers, with Homo Sapiens always caught in the middle.

Today these incompatible primate/alien genes fuel humankind's conflicts, mainly our political strife and our mental illnesses. After all, aren't we all affected by some sort of turmoil? What generates this unnatural discontent within a species?

And so, though mostly primate, the reader ought to consider the prospect of having a "bit of alien" in one's DNA—the family tree branch never mentioned!

But, as I urge, don't panic … yet.

PREFACE

History Recalibrated Upgraded Narratives

"The eyes of that species of extinct Giants, whose bones fill the mounds of America, have gazed on Niagara, as ours do now." —**Abraham Lincoln**

As the decades pass and Humankind slowly penetrates reality with more and more findings, building quasi-awareness, it behooves us to reconsider some of the staid elements of our belief systems.

For instance, at one point we needed to reevaluate our belief in a flat Earth. Contemplate another example—did the reader ever consider that the grave mounds of American giants which Lincoln mentioned still exist, and that other giants once lived as claimed in the bible and elsewhere? What genes did they possess? Ponder ...

The **Nephilim (giants)** *were in the earth in those days, and also after that, when the sons of God came into the daughters of men, and they bore children to them.* —**The Book of Genesis**.

Years ago, this old testament sentence got me going with the "just recently" and "genetic conflict" frameworks described herein. Historical writings reveal that Aliens lived as gods amongst their respective Homo Sapient workers, until one day some took a few of the women, begetting new creatures, giants, called "Nephilim" in the bible. These were not created *in vitro* under controlled conditions, but resulted from full sexual exchanges of genetic matter between the Aliens and the Homo Sapiens. Ugh!

The event occurred just before "The Flood" and I realized that, like The Flood, *Nephilim*—crossbred *Homo Sapiens* and *Aliens*—stand as just one of many unsolved historical legends we brush aside. Indeed, no orthodox researcher considers these when explaining the sudden, dramatic ascent of humankind just 6,000 years ago.

And once the mainstream deems a legend preposterous, then *the experiences actually reported by ancient people are excluded from historical consideration* ... a type of enforced ignorance. Certainly not all pre- civilization proclamations are tall tales, so... shouldn't we be doing a lot better at sorting through them by now?

Efforts to bring historical standing to mythology has advanced over the course of the author's lifetime, thanks mainly to the extraterrestrial-theory scholars (referred to later). Yet, even now, no compelling backstory reconciles competing belief systems. A percentage of people insist God held a direct hand in matters; others assume alien involvement; many believe that evolving primates drove history... with most regarding any attempt to explain our past a futile exercise. By habit, we throw up our hands, unable to connect the ancient puzzle pieces of myth, science, theology, genetics, and archeological relics into a compelling, unified history of pre-civilized humankind, 4,000 BC to 1,000 BC.

In turn, this miscalculation of genetic beginnings results in not knowing who we actually are today, and so libertarians base modern political tactics on a flawed foundation. They get drawn into diversionary ideological arguments and do not squarely face humankind's genetically determined trajectory. Most people want socialism, no questions asked, while "...those who are about to die" still desire libertarianism.

My Damascus Road Experience

An example of competing theories *leading us nowhere* finds many accepting the bible as "the word of God" with evolutionists diametrically opposed to biblical content. The naysayers see the Book of Genesis as fable. And, as fable, they assume that people such as Adam and Noah— if they indeed existed—did not actually live for 900 years. Instead, these ancient claims surely meant something else, perhaps they meant "900 months," not "900 years"? And all this talk about Sons-of-God impregnating human women causing Nephilim Giants appears even more far-fetched. Forget aliens or Sons-of-God; we evolved from apes and came out of Africa 70,000 years ago.

And as for myself?

After assuming biblical content, pagan-like, for most of my life, one day I decided to flip this mindset around. Instead of casting biblical passages as parables and fables, I instead recast them as *sincere accounts.*

As Isaac Newton suggested, I decided to look for ways—historical constructs—that would support *literal interpretation of these sincere accounts* as the most-likely explanation of what went down... and the best explanation of why we behave as we do today. I rethought many mythical topics – in context of modern knowledge - to consider if other *more likely* narratives could explain... who we are.

Could Noah Have Lived for 900 Years?

Consider below, for example, a recasting using Einsteinian physics to suggest how Noah could have lived for 900 solar years.

But please don't conclude anything just yet. This is a new and astonishing insight, outlined just to get you started, with greater discussion to follow. Using what we now know of physics, there are three retro-constructs.

Construct 1—In days past, light photons, electrons, and other *atomic activity* moved much more rapidly than now, and then decelerated as we moved away from the "Big Bang." If so, Noah's body, consisting of trillions of atoms operating closer in time to the Big Bang *likely* generated more amounts of energy *per second* than ours, keeping the ark-builder strong and healthy. Explanation ...

> The key to the "atomic speed" construct pictures the immediate instance of the "Big Bang" ... the first flash of pure expanding energy and *no* mass. With E=MC2, *when mass was zero*, light speed would need to approach infinity to offset infinite energy. This implies that since then, light and electric particle speeds have slowed from near infinity down to today's 186,000 miles-per-second rate, commensurate with the growing level of mass in the universe. Logically, deceleration continues to this day, as more and more dark matter forms (dark matter only conceptualized after Einstein posted E=MC2).
>
> And so, everything changes. Initially, when universal expansion operated *near infinity*, one billion years of electron cycles at today's "slow" electron speed only took a solar *day* for the same number of cycles to occur. Likewise, the life force 6,000 years back enjoyed the fuel of many more atomic cycling repetitions occurring each solar year than occur now.

Construct 2—This atomic multiple caused plant life on earth to soar, generating far greater amounts of oxygen than today's 21 percent level. Indeed, air bubbles trapped within old tree-resin amber show a 35 percent oxygen level. Noah's high-energy body would have had all the oxygen necessary to fuel his metabolism.

Construct 3—Also a factor for living 900 years is Noah's status as only the 10th generation since Adam. Noah's genes accumulated few mutations. Unlike today, where every mutation and accumulated viral parasite since Adam lurks within our gene pool (de-evolution), Noah had no material weaknesses. He lived life high energy, high oxygen, and free of defect.

Historical Mysteries Can Explain the Then and the Now

This framework on how to live for 900 years exists as just one spoke on the "ancient legends wheel" that begs fresh inspection...

Hence this book contemplates "What about the dinosaurs? What about giants? What about the flood? What about the races and languages? What about Moses? What about the pyramids? What about the Sumerian and Sanskrit texts, Greek, Chinese, and Mayan myths? What about the source of ideas? What about the dichotomy of Socialism versus Libertarianism, what about ..."

The overarching hypothesis adds up to *a unified theory of divine creation, natural evolution, and alien intervention,* and SUBJUGATED connects these elements, leading us from 4,000 BC to today, revealing the genetic underpinning driving our ongoing political strife. Most importantly, it explains the modern goal of exterminating those *Alien- libertarian* remnants (me), standing in the way of the *Primate-socialist* pyramid-of-control-based society, with everyone content, sitting on their assigned perch.

Most would say that this book boasts far too much ambition, covering just about everything imaginable in "just one go." But that remains the point. To sum it up, everything must hang together in a unified manner, and SUBJUGATED attempts to encapsulate the central truth of our Homo Sapient species into one cohesive narrative.

SUBJUGATED begins with the past and ends with the present, so get ready for a fast... but solid ride!

CHAPTER 1

Intervention, the Alternative History

What is Man? Man is a noisome bacillus whom Our Heavenly Father created because he was disappointed in the monkey. — **Mark Twain**

SUBJUGATED offers an alternative framework to explain biblical and other ancient passages and connects this updated framework to today's world. By looking through the combined lenses of divine creation, natural evolution, and alien intervention, we recast the competing narratives of *God micro-managing human affairs* versus *evolution occurring strictly via cellular mutations*, enabling us to ask, "What is going on here amongst these various imperfect mortal beings who suddenly took over the earth, and what are we up to now?"

As a start, if one puts on hold the mindset of God poking his nose into our petty human affairs, one might instead find advanced outside "aliens" trying out all kinds of practical, even nutty things on humans. The bible chronicles these foreign imperialistic actors as gods, devils, and angels, rather than pushy mortals from elsewhere. But once we regard mortal aliens as responsible for the ensuing nonsense, we can no longer blame God!

What mortal aliens?

The Book of Genesis mentions Nephilim, a crossbreed of humans and some "other" species from above. The Old

Testament refers to these mysterious "Others" as the "sons of God," and the Book of Enoch calls them the "Watchers." We will dig into these texts shortly, but to get you started, I re-present the aforementioned quote from the bible:

> *The Nephilim were in the earth in those days, and also after that, when the sons of God came in unto the daughters of men, and they bore children to them; the same were the mighty men that were of old, the men of renown.*

How can one brush this statement aside?

A second biblical quote follows; a report on the Nephilim giants by Joshua upon his return from a spying mission in Canaan:

> *And there we saw the Nephilim, the sons of Anak, who come of the Nephilim; and we were in our own sight as grasshoppers, and so we were in their sight.*

Apparently, these Nephilim (meaning "Giants" in Greek) came about through the crossbreeding of the Sons of God and human women, as follows:

> *Now when men began to multiply on the face of the earth and daughters were born to them, the sons of God saw that the daughters of men were beautiful, and they took as wives whomever they chose.*

Enoch—alive back then, and who we will cover later—has it that 200 or so of these Sons of God "landed" on Mount Harmon in present- day Israel, spread out, and wantonly began taking human women, impregnating them by the thousands.

Though this assault is never mentioned in churches or synagogues, theological intellectuals love to debate whether the aforementioned "Sons of God" were angels, spirits, or (human) men possessed by devils. This debate is slightly irrelevant. The birth of many crossbred Nephilim babies is what's relevant; huge babies, undoubtedly cut from their human mothers' bellies, who would mature into unstoppable sexual beasts and (unless sterile, like a mule) beget even more Nephilim babies.

What a mess.

Apparently, whoever oversaw these 200 interlopers came down hard on them and their mutinous behavior. Here the Bible's New Testament describes the "clamping down":

> *And the angels who did not stay within their own position of authority, but left their proper dwelling, he has kept in eternal chains under gloomy darkness until the judgment of the great day—just as Sodom and Gomorrah and the surrounding cities, which likewise indulged in sexual immorality and pursued unnatural desire, serve as an example by undergoing a punishment of eternal fire.*

Though punished for the crossbreeding, the horses had left the barn, so to speak, and the Homo Sapient gene pool now stood corrupted.

One certainly assumes that crossbreeding with outsiders is not good for Homo Sapiens. To start, the resultant Nephilim offspring grew into giants, seven-to-12 feet in height, and they dominated everything, possessing insatiable sex drives. Undoubtedly, the fledgling Homo Sapient species would be squeezed out were nothing done.

The Homo Sapiens, though, have a *Champion* responsible for them— labeled "God" by the bible, but in *SUBJUGATED*, this Champion exists a mere mortal alien with a big job—possibly that of a ship's Admiral— responsible for orchestrating the overall Homo Sapient experiment, now gone sour.

The *Homo Sapient* project began under his direction once the upgrade potential of the *Human* hunter/gathers became apparent. Primitive Humans functioned as capable animals, with large brains, already employing crude language, using some stone tools and crafting simple pottery, living plainly for some 200,000 years. But these attributes represented the extent of the then-current Human gene set.

Nevertheless, a simple genetic *implant* might just bring these rather dull beings up to the next level, the way today, we Homo Sapiens play with genetics to create faster horses and genetically modified "corn." The upgraded Humans could be useful, both as workers, and even as soldiers in the armies of competing Aliens.

These Aliens, who, of course, operated at much higher levels than we do even now, knew, for instance, how to power up the mind itself, not just make "corn" disease resistant. The Admiral decided to run the upgrade experiment.

Sure enough, the minds of the resulting Adam and Eve babies impressed all, but at a big cost. Unlike the human parents that sired the Adam and Eve embryos—who both looked the way all animals of a kind appear, each identical, each uniformly beautiful—these genetically modified "Homo Sapiens" all looked different. Few possessed beauty, with many of them anxious, depressed, or worse, psychopaths (no moral or emotional foundation whatsoever), prone to lying and deception.

Yes, the alien doctors knew how to infuse genes, but in doing so, they created the unintended consequence of a destabilized organism, leading to the many flawed physical and mental traits exhibited by Homo Sapiens ever since, unlike any other species on Earth.

But, as any breakfast enthusiast knows, "You can't make an omelet without breaking a few eggs," and so the Admiral kept the experiment going. Sure enough, soon Cain killed Abel, and, for some reason, the project team allowed Cain to live. Mistake upon mistake followed, with yet another mistake: the crossbred Nephilim.

After chaining his bad crew members to "hell" for the crossbreeding debacle, the Admiral, probably seeking to save his job, chose to wipe out the original *Simple Humans*, plus the *Homo Sapient Humans*, plus the vile *Nephilim Humans* by unleashing a devastating flood, leaving no loose ends. He had the technology to effect this, as the very anti-gravity system used to power his ship can repurpose to perform odd jobs on any given planet. The bible puts it this way:

> *Then the LORD saw that the wickedness of man was great upon the earth, and that every inclination of the thoughts of his heart was altogether evil all the time. And the LORD said, "I will blot out man, whom I have created, from the face of the earth—every man and beast and crawling creature and bird of the air—for I am grieved that I have made them."*

But the Admiral's lieutenants—Michael, Raphael, Uriel, and Gabriel— stepped in. All was not lost. They identified a Homo Sapient family not yet poisoned with Nephilim genes: Noah, his wife, his three sons, and his three daughters-in-law stood pure. Rather than starting from scratch after the flood, they could use this family as a quick reboot button.

Indeed, post flood, Noah's decedents started things up again, living long lives, bearing children, slowly repopulating the Tigris Euphrates Valley according to plan. Noah himself lived another 350 years!

But a problem surfaced. Unbeknownst to all, one of Noah's daughters-in-law carried buried Nephilim genes, and soon, some of her offspring yielded new generations of giants who formed kingdoms in Canaan and the surrounding areas of modern-day Israel and Jordan.

The Admiral, who came to and from Earth, operating in different time scales than those fixed on Earth, brooded over the failed flood extermination and needed a new plan. Nephilim abomination against humanity would not stand. At first, he torched two of the worst Nephilim cities, Sodom and Gomorrah, where debauchery stood as a way of life.

But too many Nephilim mixed in, requiring a more surgical approach. The Admiral hatched a second attempt at total extermination, envisioning a military force to do the heartless work. Conveniently, a potential army waited innocently in the wings, the slaves of Egypt, the Hebrews.

The Admiral assigned a trusted lieutenant to act as on-site project manager of this new approach (the lieutenant is called "the Lord" by the Hebrews). His mission? To extract this Homo Sapiens horde from Pharaoh and convert them into a military machine able to annihilate Nephilim kingdoms. Over the next 40 years of Earth time, all of the know-how and technology available from the Admiral came to bear for this extermination agenda.

With the promise of land and some very stern management oversight by the on-site lieutenant, the "chosen ones," the former slaves, followed the script, though frustrating "the Lord" every step of the way.

For decades, "the Lord," this on-site lieutenant, traveled with the Israelite horde, boasting his own camp tent (the meeting tent), his own culinary preferences, a personal guard (the Levite tribe), an ability to use gravitational disruptions (the Ark), and demonstrating the temper requisite to recondition the Hebrew population away from their habitual complaining, converting them into a killing machine.

But this assignment tasked "the Lord," and he never pulled punches:

> *The Lord said to Moses, "How long will these people treat me with contempt? How long will they refuse to believe in me, in spite of all the signs I have performed among them? I will strike them down with a plague and destroy them, but I will make you into a nation greater and stronger than they."*

In the coming chapter *The Lord*, we will closely examine how the Lord interacted with Moses, Moses's brother Aaron, and with the Hebrew military captain, Joshua. Later we will deconstruct creation statements in Genesis, factoring in the earlier-mentioned atomic speed theory, while pondering if the Lord likely dictated Genesis to Moses, "the Lord" possibly a witness to part of the Genesis "Day 6" activities.

Throughout the Lord's time with the Hebrews, the Ark's power stood central to the entire Exodus and Nephilim extermination saga. Today, we Homo Sapiens use gasoline-powered cars and dream of electric cars, proud of our underachievement. But long ago—as Sanskrit writings proclaim—Aliens had mastered the mysterious forces of gravity, using variations of anti-gravity technology to propel vehicles and even disrupt natural conditions. This tactical capability would cause frogs to leave the Nile, locusts to swarm, waters to part, quail to fly from marshes to feed the wandering Hebrews, and so on. But most of all, Aliens would use anti-gravity technology to level cities and destabilize tectonic plates.

In the end, around 1,400 BC, the Hebrews leveled 30 of 32 Nephilim kingdoms, leaving few survivors. Hence, they *almost* achieved their designated mission. But not *all* Nephilim fell. Four hundred years later, around 1,000 BC, David fought Goliath, a nine-foot tall Philistine, and so it continued. Alien genes remained on Earth.

But the Exodus books are not unique. Tales of alien "gods," themselves at war with one other, using massively destructive weaponry and Homo Sapient troops, abound in India, China, Mayan lands, North America and elsewhere.

Thus, consider this Alternative History, with a few more things to mention...

First, don't think the above a case for Atheism, the proposition that God does not exist. *SUBJUGATED* instead poses the simple proposition that although God may very well exist, *He* had nothing to do with the violent sagas of the Old Testament and at other ancient Homo Sapient outposts in Egypt, Mesopotamia, India, Greece, China, and the Americas… we just *assumed* He had. Blaming God for both the Adam & Eve and secondary Nephilim crossbreeding disasters would compare to today blaming God for the fallout from genetically modified foods, chemical carcinogens, and pollution. *He* didn't do it.

Nor should the reader assume *SUBJUGATED* a case pitting the competing theories of evolution and divine creation against one other.

Evolution and divine creation have nothing to do with what went down once things got rolling during the times of Adam, Enoch, Noah, Abraham, Moses, and Joshua, nor do creation/evolution theories have anything to do with the current troubles of the Homo Sapient race.

Instead, the biblical players of old are mere Alien and Homo Sapient mortals playing out their destinies using the cards dealt: a new Homo Sapient species just getting started, interacting with superior foreign overlords who possess vast stores of know-how. Together they muddle through the grand Homo Sapient experiment, an experiment that went haywire, requiring repair.

It was never repaired. At some point, the Homo Sapiens were abandoned, and we now crawl all over the planet, eight billion of us— the only species, other than domesticated animals—where everyone looks different. In *Subjugated Volume III – Genetics Drive Political Orientation,* we will unravel how our unnatural genetic makeup has brought us to a final extermination conflict.

One more thing. Nephilim lived elsewhere, whether migrating from the mid-east to other parts of the world or sired by outsiders on diverse continents. This will be covered in the *Evidence from Other Civilizations* chapter, and in the *Bigfoot, Little People and Ohio Giants* sections.

For example, thousands of giant skeletons found in North America during the 1800's cannot be explained. Where did they come from and how and why were these American giants exterminated... and by whom? Likewise, the Incas—who could not write and had not "discovered" the wheel—told the Spanish that giants from a previous era had built the gigantic stone structures found in South America. Considering the relative lack of giants today, it appears most were killed off, but also, as described in the *Genetics chapter,* the Nephilim genes were probably recessive, so that over time, the traits fizzled out of the Homo Sapient population.

As said, it all happened just recently, and not as told. Ok, here goes... step it up!

CHAPTER 2

Homo Sapiens, How Old Are We?

I am quite sure that our views on evolution would be very different had biologists studied genetics and natural selection before and not after most of them were convinced that evolution had occurred. —**John B. Haldane, British Genetics Pioneer**

Evolutionists believe that humans have evolved forever, with new versions of "us" bubbling up across the ages, each up-and-coming revision incrementally smarter, nobler, and better than the previous edition. They claim today's Human genetically equal to the Humans coming out of Africa 70,000 years ago, we just know more now.

In contrast, religious adherents believe that God created Humans on Day 6, perfect from the get-go, made in *His* image.

Evolutionists pitch "natural selection"— millions of spontaneous cellular mutations occurring over millions of years, some beneficial, others not, whose collective randomness somehow spawn new species. With natural selection, Homo Sapiens traits such as literature and engineering came about by cellular mutation 200,000 years ago—it just took a while for humans to realize they had these abilities.

Yet one ponders, even assuming *incremental evolution* plausible, does it explain Homo Sapiens intellect, and why it took 200,000 years to kick into gear?

Homo Sapiens—the ones who behave like us, *who foster civilizations*— have a mere record of only 6,000 years, if that. Civilized beings on Earth, the ones who manage nature rather than have nature manage them, are truly a new phenomenon. All other animals passively exist in specific biospheres, merely reproducing (think sea turtles or cavemen) with some variations occurring *within* each species, but only to help specimens better cope with the *local* environment controlling them. Mankind's intellectual leap, operating above nature and possessing traits needed for civilized society, travel beyond the scope of *incremental evolution*.

Biblical creationists explain this unprecedented leap of brain power simply by crediting God for the advanced traits of mankind, an easy out.

Still, a third door exists called *intervention*, a door that most people do not dare to open. Behind it lie ancient manuscripts, such as the Hebrew bible, the Sumerian clay tablets, the Indian Sanskrit records, and many stone carvings showing "gods" teaching humans, "gods" in flying vehicles, and etchings of "humans" with oblong heads, not appearing of the primate branch.

This assortment of tangible historical relics argues in favor of disruption of the usual, slow-moving trajectory of evolution, and that intervention *likely* explains our sudden ascent.

Below I list the first human civilizations. I contend that what preceded these might have been *Simple Human*, but not *Homo Sapient Human*, that is, *not yet having a civilization-oriented intellect*. So, what went down? How, without warning, did we jump from our existence as Simple Humans using stone tools and primitive pottery, to become Homo Sapiens, the "wise ones," suddenly able to form civilizations, to write and accrue knowledge, to build buildings, cities, and much more? Here are the founders:

    2,200 BC - The Mesopotamians
    2,200 BC - The Indus Peoples
    2,200 BC - The Egyptians
    2,200 BC - The Chinese

These blossomed all at once, and other than cuneiform tablets, the most vivid literary record of early humanity is the bible, putting Adam at around 4,000 BC, and Noah's flood at around 2,400 BC. The above civilizations all came around 200 years post-flood.

So, allowing for some wiggle-room with dimensional dates, it appears that Homo Sapient intellect showed itself in Adam's time, around 4,000 BC, and that Homo Sapient civilization started after the 2,400 BC flood, only blossoming around 2,200 BC., and that before Adam, only crude hunter/gatherer stone tools and pottery existed, nothing else.

Creationists claim nothing came before Adam, not even pottery, sticking with *God made man on the sixth day*, as if that covers it all.

Evolutionists postulate that humans *just like us* existed before civilizations formed—primitive yet whole—first reproducing as simple hunter/gatherers for some 130,000 years in Africa, before spreading across the earth 70,000 years ago. I'm not sure where they get these dates, as carbon 14 dating (upon which half-life calibrations can be made) is good for just a few thousand years before all the carbon 14 is gone. Most people do not know that about carbon 14 dating, and actually accept the dates given!

But more to the point, even after accepting the made-up dates, evolutionists never discuss why we suddenly moved beyond *environmentally-controlled hunter/gathering* to become builders of cities. They only mentioned *evolution*, as if that covers it all. It covers nothing!

Evolutionists construct various scenarios; consider this one: rather than spending hours gnawing raw food, humans discovered fire, allowing them to cook, requiring smaller "mutated" intestines to digest their food, thereby diverting more body-wide energy to the brain, while also providing more time to think. And with these advantages, humans eventually sorted out calculus, eventually leading to our aerospace program. This is the better-food/more-time evolution theory.

I contend that both the creationist and the evolutionist have quirky, incomplete explanations with many holes and ignored puzzle pieces. SUBJUGATED argues that an interventionist element, a third factor, must account for the sudden appearance of "us," describing who we are, how we "got here" so abruptly, why we behave the way we do today, perpetually upset and at each other's throats.

As you will see, we appear an experiment conducted by outsiders, an experiment that went wrong, with the interlopers ultimately abandoning us. Evidence for intervention appears throughout the bible and in many other ancient sources as well. To get a handle, we will deconstruct the historical record, using interventionist findings to plug evolutionist/ creationist narrative shortcomings.

For example, everyone knows the story of David killing the giant Goliath with a slingshot. The bible describes Goliath as so many cubits in height, which yields nine and one-half feet on today's scale.

But the truth surrounding the saga dwarfs this single incident. The big story: Goliath possessed non-human genes, part human and part something else, making him a crossbreed. Similar to mating a horse and a donkey to make a mule, the bible calls these human crossbreeds "Nephilim," and they stood from seven to 12 feet in height.

As already mentioned, Nephilim, *according to the bible*, were sired by extraterrestrial fathers, the "Sons of God" before the time of Noah, around 3,000 BC. Supposedly destroyed by the 2,400 BC flood, by 2,300 BC the Nephilim returned, forming kingdoms in the current region of Jordan and Israel. Nephilim sects included the Amorites, the Canaanites, the Philistines (Goliath's "people"), and others.

By 1,000 BC, when David killed Goliath, the Israelites had been at war with Nephilim populations for 400 years. One might even say that the Israelites were "chosen" by an interventionist (not God) to fight and exterminate these giants. *Chosen*, as, after all, Moses left Egypt by the interventionist command of "the Lord" and while wandering the desert "the Lord" *chose* Moses to prepare the Hebrews for eventual warfare against the Nephilim in the promised land.

Joshua, *chosen* by the Lord to succeed Moses, conducted the actual battles, exterminating untold thousands of Nephilim, though some obviously slipped through, surviving hundreds of years at least until the David and Goliath era. Later, we'll look at "the Lord" through interventionist glasses.

One might notice that although biblical, none of this Nephilim business is spoken about in Jewish synagogues or Christian churches.

Instead, organized religions channel parishioners into dissecting isolated sentences of the bible, hunting for God's message, not seeing the forest for the trees. But if instead one reads the full texts, supposedly formulated by Moses and Joshua, all of this gritty history describing human origins, its aberrant offshoots, and its interventionist agents lies apparent.

Parallel to religious decoying, evolutionists also lead us by the nose, having us look at old monkey bones, making us believe our human traits accrued bit-by-bit through endless micro-cell mutations.

To protect their fragile dogmas, both evolutionist and creationists battle the other to hoard the *sole* explanation of mankind, with each camp covering up their respective narrative's shortcomings.

And yet by all counts, human blossoming, *the formation of civilization and the accumulation of know-how,* started suddenly around 2,300 BC, a telltale clue that intervention occurred. All written accounts point to this, yet evolutionists willfully ignore the coincidence, and religious minds skillfully chase isolated bible passages, neither school embracing the full recordings of the ancients.

Besides the bible, other rare histories exist for us to tap into, such as the Sumerian tablets and the Indian Sanskrit writings. These speak of a unique time when post-flood peoples—yes, around 2,200 BC—were suddenly enlightened, taught things, and guided by other beings. We will look at these writings later.

The Sumerian/Indian/Chinese accounts and their carved stone works, plus the accounts and works of many others, must be considered in conjunction with the Jewish bible to form a more complete picture of the pre-flood *dawn* of mankind and the post-flood *awakening* of mankind. Undoubtedly, outsiders interfered in the pre-flood period, boosting human IQ, and in the post-flood years they taught these brainy-but-ignorant Homo Sapiens how to build civilizations, only to abandon humanity at some point.

Recall that the written accounts and physical works of many civilizations portray giants, visiting gods, and air travel occurring around the time mankind started to civilize. These will come into play.

And finally, realizing both dull primitive Humans and advanced Homo Sapiens quite adept at eliminating other species, the biblically documented Israelite assault on the Nephilim kingdoms demands a better explanation than *a wandering people finally reach the land of milk and honey.* We will examine the need in 1,400 BC to cull the Nephilim giants, as well as the drive today to exterminate a minority of Homo Sapiens who still exhibit Alien traits.

CHAPTER 3

Prove It!
History Requires Imagination

"About the time of the end, a body of men will be raised up who will turn their attention to the Prophecies, and in the midst of much clamor and opposition insist upon their literal interpretation." – **Sir Isaac Newton**

Please do not assume SUBJUGATED to assert proof of extraterrestrial involvement with mankind, any more than Darwin claimed proof of Evolution. SUBJUGATED offers something more realistic, the *plausibility* of extraterrestrial involvement.

Over the years, authors such as *Erich Von Daniken*, who, in the 1960's, first floated aspects of the intervention theory with his *Chariots of Fire* book, have been ridiculed and dismissed by critics who cite the evidence offered as misinterpretation or that other explanations exist or that the good evidence still does not amount to proof. Using dismissal tactics, evolutionists and creationists avoid the evidential challenge these ancient relics represent, thus sticking to their own unsupported theories.

Philosophers label this a *sophist* trick, as nothing can be proven when it comes right down to it. Descartes at least came up with what is called an *a priori*, self-evident logic proof, such as A = A, and, "I think, therefore I am." Scientists say that scientific proof occurs when a physical result occurs over and over without exception, such as all objects falling at 32 feet-per-second^2. Lawyers speak of "beyond a reasonable doubt" levels of courtroom proof.

Historical proof, though, proves more elusive, not truly possible, especially in the pre-writing era. Only religious and scientific *doctrine protectors* demand absolute historical proof when asked to abandon their versions.

But we are not claiming absolute proof in this document. If you don't like certain bits of evidence or logic, then dismiss these, but piecemeal refutations do not sanctify unfounded trust in creation or evolution explanations, both failing to address many loose ends, therefore lacking unity.

Instead, here we contemplate how best to understand our sudden ascent with the "most-likely" unified explanation, and for a theory to be likely, requires the presentation of some compelling *evidence* and *logic* to explain the phenomenon under consideration.

In the case of evolution, no hard *evidence* exists to prove that new species come about through collective cellular mutations. None. Evolution's *logic* builds from the observation that mutations occur, which leads to the *possibility* that, given time, new species *might form* via collective mutations. Not proven, but it can ring true if not looking closely. But even if true, cumulative mutations do not explain how human hunter/gatherers, using stone tools and making crude pottery, suddenly built cities around 2,200 BC.

Evolution's incremental, long-term construct negates itself as the answer to the *historical suddenness* this book seeks to untangle. Evolution offers no hard evidence, and its long-term approach does not even apply within this suddenness conundrum.

As with evolution, *biblical creation* offers no direct *evidence* proving this the way things happened. Instead, creation's *logic* asserts *divinity* essential, as the universe's complexity begs for a divine mind capable of creating it—a circular argument. But even assuming creation via a deity necessary, this does not dictate deterministic micro-management of every detail by the creator. Other intelligent-design-like natural forces, including physics, chemistry, and evolution manage details. Certainly, God is not party to the price of gold. He created E=MC2, and every other concept and formula out there. And creation need not adhere to a schedule, done in six days, but it can be achieved *through* time, the way I'm creating this manuscript as I type. Creation can also include interventions that cause sharp turns, such as when Europeans arrived in America, or with Aliens arriving from elsewhere.

Intervention, though, boasts substantial evidence, both written and literally in stone, and considerable logic to account for the instantaneous step-up of Humans becoming Homo Sapiens. Intervention can speak to how for hundreds of thousands of years, we lived like the other animals locked in nature, until suddenly we behaved as Homo Sapiens, able to accumulate know-how, build civilizations, and control nature itself. *Intervention* is simply the more-likely explanation to complete the puzzle, especially as creationism and evolution, though both partially correct in their respective domains, offer nothing to explain the recent, explosive Homo Sapient phenomenon.

And, *intervention* adds up to one thing: we are part advanced Alien and part simple Human, and as you will see in the *Plato* Chapter, those pining for primate-side domination must obscure this dualism, to return to primate-styled socialism. Hence socialists cling to evolution to explain us. Evolution sidesteps the obvious: that many of our foundation traits are not of this Earth.

And with these introductory remarks made, I invite you to explore, not scoff at, *intervention*, the third leg of the creation, evolution and intervention stool. But first, meet Moses and "the Lord."

CHAPTER 4

Moses & "the Lord"... Partners

This chapter will use excerpts from the first books of the bible to describe "The Lord." Before one might accept that our Homo Sapient behavior stems from genetic unbalance, one must first conclude that our unbalanced selves were not "made" on Day 6 by God. The various chapters in SUBJUGATED dealing with the books of the bible are here for that purpose.

The first five books of the bible—*GENESIS, EXODUS, LEVITICUS, NUMBERS, DEUTERONOMY*—are called The Torah, said to be the Laws of God as revealed to Moses. Whether or not Moses wrote them down or memorized revelations, later telling them to other rabbis for posterity, is not known. He probably wrote them down, as Moses, an Egyptian prince and one of Pharaoh's great warriors (covered later), came out of Egypt, a semi-literate society. The five books contain vast hard-to-memorize detail as to dialogues that once took place, and the likelihood that Moses learned the history of humankind—*GENESIS*— from his alien mentors also comes later in this work.

The Torah, though, reads more like Moses's camp journal, starting from his first meeting with "the Lord" in Egypt and running until Moses's death 40 years later. Upon the death of Moses, Joshua assumed the journalistic responsibilities with, appropriately, *The Book of Joshua,* describing the conquest of the 32 Canaanite kingdoms. With "the Lord" in tow, similar to Moses, Joshua is provisioned with all the "Lord-like" weapons for which one could hope.

The only non-journal aspect of all the writings is GENESIS, as GENESIS, the first book, took place before Moses's time. Someone must have provided Moses with all the detail, including the actual words spoken by the likes of Adam and Eve, Noah, and Abraham. Most true believers assume that Moses received the GENESIS "backstory" through divine revelation from GOD while up on Mount Sinai.

Others say ancient luminaries wrote the stories on cuneiform clay tablets that survived into Moses's time. Still others claim that priests wrote all of the Torah between the time of David in 900 BC and the Babylonian captivity in 500 BC, suggesting it was all made up.

But a more likely source of the GENESIS backstory is that "the Lord," who, for decades, traveled everywhere with Moses, and regularly conversed with him at the "meeting tent," explained creation in detail to Moses, as the Lord possessed firsthand knowledge of the actual process.

Functionally, I describe the Lord as "the onsite project manager," assigned to Earth, working on the Nephilim Extermination project. The Lord, apparently, dwelled in a vessel hovering over a pillar of smoke and fire, set above the meeting tent. The Lord undoubtedly reported to higher-ups, and I call his boss "The Admiral"—the guy running the whole Earth operation.

For the reader to get a feel for this alternative picture suggesting the Torah as basically a journal of camp life, consider some of the mundane dialogue between the Lord and Moses...

> The Lord called to Moses and spoke to him from the tent of meeting. He said, "Speak to the Israelites and say to them: 'When anyone among you brings an offering to the Lord, bring as your offering an animal from either the herd or the flock.' If the offering is a burnt offering from the herd, you are to offer a

male without defect. You must present it at the entrance to the tent of meeting so that it will be acceptable to the Lord ..."

The micromanagement boggles the mind. Below, "the Lord" speaks to Moses and Aaron while still in Egypt regarding portions of lamb:

This month is to be for you the first month, the first month of your year. Tell the whole community of Israel that on the tenth day of this month each man is to take a lamb for his family, one for each household. If any household is too small for a whole lamb, they must share one with their nearest neighbor, having taken into account the number of people there are. You are to determine the amount of lamb needed in accordance with what each person will eat.

Further, while in the Sanai desert, "the Lord" proclaimed:

If you bring a grain offering baked in an oven, it is to consist of the finest flour: either thick loaves made without yeast and with olive oil mixed in or thin loaves made without yeast and brushed with olive oil.

Pages and pages of food preparation proclamations by "the Lord" exist; the above is just an isolated sentence.

Separate from these incidental meeting tent conversations about food stands the singular Mount Sinai experience. What took place up on Sinai actually appears more like revelation, and less like camp talk. After all, after Moses went up to the mountain, he came back down with a burnt face. This never happened when discussing food preparation matters with "the Lord."

One can surmise that up on the mountain Moses met the higher authority, i.e., the Admiral, the boss of the extermination exercise, the one who knew the whole story from Adam onward. The Admiral, who reported to a home planet probably tiring of the whole Homo Sapient debacle, needed to look Moses in the eye, and set parameters for the venture ahead, the planned invasion of Nephilim territories.

It was a lot for Moses to take in, but because Moses and "the Lord" spoke all the time at the meeting tent, with "the Lord" fully versed in creation astrophysics, with an all-to-clear understanding of the whole Nephilim backstory and the upcoming mission to exterminate Nephilim, well... "the Lord" probably served as a good editor for Moses as he compiled the segments of GENESIS.

Basically, at the special status meeting up on the mountain, "The Admiral" gave the 10 Commandments to Moses so that the Israelites would *not* adopt the sacrilegious behavior of the Canaanite Nephilim. After all, the Nephilim way of life—complete debauchery—might appeal to some of the Hebrew men. "The Lord," operating the camp, had to ensure the enforcement of the Commandments, hence:

> *The Lord said to Moses, "Speak to the Israelites and say to them: 'I am the Lord. You must not do as they do in Egypt, where you used to live, and you must not do as they do in the land of Canaan, where I am bringing you. Do not follow their practices. You must obey my laws and be careful to follow my decrees. I am the Lord. Keep my decrees and laws, for the person who obeys them will live by them. I am the Lord.'"*

After 40 days up on Mount Sinai, Moses came down to face the worst possible outcome: his people had created a golden calf to worship, identical to those the sacrilegious Nephilim Canaanites worshipped.

If the Israelites could worship a cow, they could easily adopt every other bad habit taught by Nephilim society. So, to instill discipline in the Israelites, the "on-site Lord" must quickly instill a fear of his ruthlessness in curbing bad behavior and bad attitude.

Below, as example, out in the Sinai desert, "the Lord" punishes a few Israelites who have gone astray:

> *The people complained about their hardships in the hearing (proximity) of the Lord, and when he (the Lord) heard them his anger was aroused. Then fire from the Lord burned among them and consumed some of the outskirts of the camp. When the people cried out to Moses, he prayed to the Lord and the fire died down.*

This kind of thing occurred rather regularly. Someone messed up. "The Lord" freaked out. Moses went in to restore peace.

But more baffling is why "the Admiral" and "the Lord" needed to recruit the Hebrews in the first place. The list of Egyptian plagues that these mysterious ones delivered with the snap of a finger makes you wonder, why didn't they simply destroy the Nephilim directly, rather than go through all of this manipulation? Why engage in all the cajoling, scheming, and detailed instruction that "the Lord" exhibited in directing Moses, aged 80, and Moses's 83-year old brother, Aaron?

Below "the Lord" assigns Moses and Aaron the important job of counting able-bodied men for the army, which either assumes "the Lord" did not know the number already, or that he needed Moses and Aaron to experience the process. "The Lord" goes so far as to pick the men he wants assigned to this project:

> *The Lord spoke to Moses in the tent of meeting in the Desert of Sinai on the first day of the second month of the second year after the Israelites came out of Egypt. He said: "Take a census of the whole Israelite community by their clans and families, listing every man by name, one by one. You and Aaron are to count according to their divisions all the men in Israel who are twenty years old or more and able to serve in the army. One man from each tribe, each of them the head of his family, is to help you.*

These are the names of the men who are to assist you:

from Reuben, Elizur son of Shedeur;

from Simeon, Shelumiel son of Zurishaddai;

from Judah, Nahshon son of Amminadab;

from Issachar, Nethanel son of Zuar;

from Zebulun, Eliab son of Helon;

from the sons of Joseph:

from Ephraim, Elishama son of Ammihud;

from Manasseh, Gamaliel son of Pedahzur;

from Benjamin, Abidan son of Gideoni;

from Dan, Ahiezer son of Ammishaddai;

from Asher, Pagiel son of Okran;

from Gad, Eliasaph son of Deuel;

from Naphtali, Ahira son of Enan."

This type of detail is astonishing, and it goes on for pages and pages, book after book, subject after subject. Below one finds just part of "the Lord's" instructions for skin disease:

> *A man who has lost his hair and is bald is clean. If he has lost his hair from the front of his scalp and has a bald forehead, he is clean. But if he has a reddish-white sore on his bald head or forehead, it is a defiling disease breaking out on his head or forehead. The priest is to examine him, and if the swollen sore on his head or forehead is reddish-white like a defiling skin disease, the man is diseased and is unclean. The priest shall pronounce him unclean because of the sore on his head.*

> *Anyone with such a defiling]disease must wear torn clothes, let their hair be unkempt, cover the lower part of their face and cry out, "Unclean! Unclean!" As long as they have the disease they remain unclean. They must live alone; they must live outside the camp.*

Consider this: After Aaron's sons were burned to death by "the Lord" for approaching "the Lord" incorrectly, Aaron, as father, also found himself on the hot seat, rebuked in detail, as follows:

> The Lord spoke to Moses after the death of the two sons of Aaron who died when they approached the Lord. The Lord said to Moses: "Tell your brother Aaron that he is not to come whenever he chooses into the Most Holy Place behind the curtain in front of the atonement cover on the ark, or else he will die.

The Wizard of Oz implied the same for Dorothy.

At some point, "the Lord" decided to create a personal staff to tend to the meeting tent, the tabernacle, the Ark of the Covenant, and "the Lord's" meals. "The Lord" chose the tribe of Levi for this role, and thereafter, the Levite men took charge of "the Lord's" stuff, including transporting it once the Israelites were on the move. The other tribes paid a tax to "the Lord" to support the Levites, as the Levites no longer had their own flocks. In getting this arrangement going, "the Lord" seemed to impose a trade of sorts with Moses:

> The Lord also said to Moses "I have taken the Levites from among the Israelites in place of the first male offspring of every Israelite woman. The Levites are mine, for all the firstborn are mine. When I struck down all the firstborn in Egypt, I set apart for myself every firstborn in Israel, whether human or animal. They are to be mine. I am the Lord."

I guess "the Lord" wanted no backtalk about getting a personal staff, and pointed out that when all of the Egyptian firstborn babies were killed, their Hebrew counterparts were spared, thus "You guys owe me!" Once he had a staff, the Lord spoke with further precision:

Bring you clear oil of pressed olives for the light so that the lamps may be kept burning continually. Outside the curtain that shields the ark of the covenant law in the tent of meeting, Aaron is to tend the lamps before the Lord from evening till morning, continually. This is to be a lasting ordinance for the generations to come. The lamps on the pure gold lampstand before the Lord must be tended continually.

"The Lord" also got involved in family squabbles. Below, a full passage showing the methods of "the Lord" in action:

Miriam and Aaron began to talk against Moses because of his Cushite wife, for he had married a Cushite (an African). "Has the Lord spoken only through Moses?" they asked. "Hasn't he also spoken through us?" And the Lord heard this.

At once the Lord said to Moses, Aaron and Miriam, "Come out to the tent of meeting, all three of you." So, the three of them went out. Then the Lord came down in a pillar of cloud; he stood at the entrance to the tent and summoned Aaron and Miriam. When the two of them stepped forward, he said, "Listen to my words:

"When there is a prophet among you, I, the Lord, reveal myself to them in visions, I speak to them in dreams.

But this is not true of my servant Moses; he is faithful in all my house.

With him I speak face to face, clearly and not in riddles; he sees the form of the Lord. Why then were you not afraid to speak against my servant Moses?" The anger of the Lord burned against them, and he left them.

When the cloud lifted from above the tent, Miriam's skin was leprous — it became as white as snow. Aaron turned toward her and saw that she had a defiling skin disease, and he said to Moses, "Please, my lord, I ask you not to hold against us the sin we have so foolishly committed. Do not let her be like a stillborn infant coming from its mother's womb with its flesh half eaten away."

So Moses cried out to the Lord, "Please, God, heal her!"

The Lord replied to Moses, "If her father had spit in her face, would she not have been in disgrace for seven days? Confine her outside the camp for seven days; after that she can be brought back." So Miriam was confined outside the camp for seven days, and the people did not move on until she was brought back.

One major element of the whole "Lord" saga is that Moses was not to live long enough to lead the people into the promised land, not due to old age, but as punishment for doubting the Lord. It all came about due to the "water from the rock" incident, though I can see nothing wrong in anything Moses did. Here is the event:

Then came the children of Israel, even the whole congregation, into the desert of Zin in the first month: and the people abode in Kadesh; and Miriam died there, and was buried there.

And there was no water for the congregation: and they gathered themselves together against Moses and against Aaron.

And the people chode with Moses, and spake, saying, Would God that we had died when our brethren died before the Lord!

And why have ye brought up the congregation of the Lord into this wilderness, that we and our cattle should die there?

And wherefore have ye made us to come up out of Egypt, to bring us in unto this evil place? It is no place of seed, or of figs, or of vines, or of pomegranates; neither is there any water to drink.

And Moses and Aaron went from the presence of the assembly unto the door of the tabernacle of the congregation, and they fell upon their faces: and the glory of the Lord appeared unto them.

And the Lord spake unto Moses, saying,

Take the rod, and gather thou the assembly together, thou, and Aaron thy brother, and speak ye unto the rock before their eyes; and it shall give forth his water, and thou shalt bring forth to them water out of the rock: so thou shalt give the congregation and their beasts drink.

And Moses took the rod from before the Lord, as he commanded him.

And Moses and Aaron gathered the congregation together before the rock, and he said unto them, "Hear now, ye rebels; must we fetch you water out of this rock?"

And Moses lifted up his hand, and with his rod he smote the rock twice: and the water came out abundantly, and the congregation drank, and their beasts also.

And the Lord spake unto Moses and Aaron. Because ye believed me not, to sanctify me in the eyes of the children of Israel, therefore ye shall not bring this congregation into the land which I have given them.

Oh well, the Lord must just have had his own reasons...

This, then, finishes "The Lord," the on-site "Project Manager" chapter. But stay tuned, for in the later *Moses Moves East* and *Joshua Conquers Canaan* chapters, "the Lord" returns, along with Moses and Joshua. But the above should get you wondering "Was the Lord 'God,' or simply the on-site project manager?"

CHAPTER 5

Genetics, Accounting for Sudden Change

Meet the Nephilim: The worst neighbors possible! In order to gauge the meaning of Adam & Eve and then the Nephilim, both exhibiting genetic traits not present in any prior Earth species, we need to dig deeper into genetics, first to envision how a genetic upgrade could be possible, and second, to contrast the great competing theories of Creation, Evolution, and Intervention to see which theory best explains these anomalies.

The introduction to this book made a point of not picking a winner between the evolutionists and the creationists. Instead, two of the book's many mysteries, Adam & Eve and the Nephilim sagas, pose interventionist breeding as more likely explanations. Interestingly, evolutionists, creationists, and interventionists all happen to share the topic of genetics.

The difference? Evolutionists claim genes mutate over time to form new species; creationists believe that each plant or animal type holds a relatively fixed genetic makeup that can vary; and interventionists deduce that only outside intervention can explain sudden, *dramatic* genetic diversions. Let's start with Adam & Eve. Where did they—or the first Homo Sapiens—come from?

According to *creationists*, GOD created man and woman instantly on Day 6, with Adam and Eve possessing a full set of Homo Sapient genes.

According to *evolutionists*, Humans instead progressed through an evolving chain of primates over millions of years via an endless string of genetic mutations.

Before getting to the third possible factor in generating a new species—intervention—let's look at the big problems with both of the first two options.

With *evolution,* one must explain how mutations in the primate world led to our vast array of intellectual faculties. Yes, chimps use sticks to pry into ant colony mounds, a skill used to obtain a crunchy snack, perhaps, but certainly not a foundation trait able to suddenly mutate into algebra, engineering, chemistry, weapon design, cuisine, etc. Realistically, no core traits exist poised within the primate chain to mutate into the vast list of human faculties. And, more so, who was our predecessor primate, the one who could count, but not do algebra? The *absence of previous traits* is the first gaping hole in a "pure evolution" explanation.

Second, if Humans blossomed 200,000 years ago already in possession of our intellect, then why did it take 200,000 years to begin behaving as we do, controlling nature, accumulating know-how, building cities and civilization structures? Instead, these Humans stayed more or less primate-like. *Stagnation* is the second hole.

This leads to the third gaping hole, the obligation to explain *the massive level of successful mutations needed* in order to jump the immediately prior primate-human species up to our current civilization-oriented level Homo Sapient species. A huge jump, at that. Most cellular mutations end up with a dying cell, as the original cell's gene/switch configuration no longer supports intact operational balance. The jump described would require untold numbers of neuron mutations, all successful, all codependent, in a single instance. *Evolution does not work that way.*

A fourth gaping hole finds no predecessor species that could have mutated. Other than Neanderthals, we have *no sign whatsoever of an immediate prior species* that could mutate into humans. We are only offered monkey bones going back millions of years. Let's consider Neanderthals to make this point clearer.

According to *evolutionists*, Neanderthals lived for hundreds of thousands of years, eventually killed off by the new aggressive Humans. Based upon genetic testing of frozen Neanderthal flesh, today's Homo Sapiens contain remnants of Neanderthal DNA (<1%), suggesting that some minor cross breeding took place once the two species confronted each other. Neanderthals certainly did not mutate into Humans where every gene in the Neanderthal system simultaneously mutated.

But as distant as Neanderthals were to human DNA, consider that across hundreds of thousands of years, Neanderthals never advanced. As with all other animals living *within nature*, they sat stagnant. They used the same five or six stone tools in 40,000 BC that they used in 250,000 BC. And Neanderthal possessed larger brains than ours, so why were they so dull, and why are we so smart? Evolutionists ignore this.

Compare both the Neanderthal and Primate-Human stagnations to the trajectory of Homo Sapiens inventiveness: can one seriously claim that our intellectual faculties resulted from unprecedented, massive, synchronized mutations from some prior primate, when no foundation intellectual traits able to be mutated can be found in any such primate?

Finally, fifth, say one day a mutated child was born with the evolved intellectual capabilities possessed by modern *Homo Sapiens*. How would this brilliance be passed along to all the slower *Humans* who had populated the world over the 70,000 years prior? Did all the Humans mutate together allowing, for example, pyramid building to take place on all continents? Checkmate?

Why is evolution even considered?

Now the *creationists* have a few issues of their own with humans popping into existence on Day 6, and they solve their issues in the most amazing ways...

For example, we only properly fathomed dinosaur bones in the mid- 1800's. Once uncovered, and the vast sets of dinosaur species identified, this new puzzle piece somehow needed to factor into the "God created everything in six days" system.

The *creationist response?* Dinosaurs lived with humans, but Noah did not invite them onto the Ark, hence they went down with the flood. Yes, creationists actually go with this, and, as you will find in Chapter 9— Noah, *they may have a case!* According to GENESIS, "all flesh became corrupted..." and for thousands of years, readers assumed this passage to mean human flesh, as contaminated with alien bloodlines. But to answer the dinosaur challenge, it became a blanket statement meaning all animal flesh became corrupted, requiring destruction, though some of the animals, obviously viewed as good, gained a seat on the Ark.

Phew, that explains it!

Adam & Eve, or whoever the first super-intelligent humans were, defy the theories of both evolutionists (mutations) and creationists (human mental illnesses). Now let's look into the likelihood of intervention by first reviewing genetics.

Basically, a species, e.g., Homo Sapiens, Cats, or Dogs, has a relatively fixed, superset set of genes, with individual genes switched on or off in various combinations to form cell types.

For example, cat heart and cat bone cells hold the same gene set, but their respective genes are switched differently to *express* the functional cat heart and bone attributes.

Likewise, our human bodies, comprising more than 100 types of cells, present a standard collection of human genes *expressed via switch combinations* to meet the role of each type of cell.

The on/off gene switching potential is vast, some of it fixed, and some of it done in real-time in response to environmental and hormonal stimulus. It is said that human genes for eye color contain dozens of options, and that one's actual expressed color comes from the color switch assigned at one's conception (not the gene, but the switch).

In this instance, based upon the parent's switch settings for eye color—plus a determination as to which parental settings are dominant or recessive—the fetus inherits its color from these parental switch preferences. Internally, humans are fundamentally the same, with each human carrying a spectrum of human eye color possibilities; the switches, not the gene itself, cause the specific outcome.

We can find another example in breeding dogs. One looks for desired traits, and then mates male and female candidates exhibiting these traits so that the switches their offspring inherit trigger the desired trait. But all dogs still carry the basic spectrum of dog trait possibilities. And so, a Chihuahua (with help) can mate with a Great Dane. Some minor mutations can also be in play, but they do not alter the dog "type."

Out in nature a similar thing occurs, called *Variation Within a Species due to Natural Selection*. Darwin sorted this out while sailing around the Galapagos Islands. He observed the same bird species having longer or shorter beaks based upon the island environment it inhabited. But beak size remains just another switch-setting option within that species.

On "Island X," rather than a breeder choosing traits, a survival advantage for birds with longer beaks causes longer-beaked birds to survive and then mate, causing Island X offspring to inherit the longer- beak *switch settings*.

Conversely, "Island Y" birds, which fare better with shorter beaks, inherit shorter-beak *switch settings* from parents thriving in this preferred shorter-beak setting.

But, as in the dog-breeding situation, all birds of that species carry genes supporting both longer and shorter beaks; beak length is just a parameter determined by a *switch setting*. Read the following report coming out of the University of Washington in 2012:

> *The locations of millions of DNA 'switches' that dictate how, when, and where in the body different genes turn on and off have been identified by a research team led by the University of Washington in Seattle. Genes make up only 2 percent of the human genome and were easy to spot, but the on/off switches controlling those genes were encrypted within the remaining 98 percent of the genome. Without these switches, called regulatory DNA, genes are inert.*

Creationists insist that God, in *His* wisdom, provided the plant and animal types with these switch options to help the individual specimens adapt to environmental fluctuations. But, mind you, in the creationist camp, God fixed the plant and animal types up-front, with new gene types not possible.

Conversely, in addition to switch options, *evolutionists* believe that although most cell mutations are minor, that some are not, and that over time, certain *mutation sequences* can lead to improved or sometimes degenerated gene types, e.g., bad eyesight.

So far, even though we humans have come a long way in understanding genetics—having created many, many breeds over the past few thousand years—humbly, we have not taken the possibilities of genetics that far. We only play with the switches. To breed animals and agricultural plants, we orchestrate desired switch combinations, *but no one has ever altered the foundation genes to create a new species.*

Currently, we are deconstructing the gene universe to catalogue all the traits expressed by individual strands of DNA within the genes, even identifying some gene conditions as participants in disease.

For example, a woman with an imperfect BRCA gene (a mutation), has a greater chance of breast cancer because the BRCA gene's job is to manufacture a protein that repairs damaged DNA before the damage leads to a cancer mutation during cell division. Inferior BRCA means that DNA breaks go unrepaired, resulting in greater opportunity for cancerous mutation.

And yes, we can pass mutations like BRCA down to future generations, thereby making offspring both stronger and weaker, i.e., evolution can also weaken us, but the question remains: do mutations lead to a fundamentally different (new) type of plant or animal?

Although mankind is getting closer to cataloguing gene pool functionality, no one out there is inventing brand new genes capable of introducing breakthrough traits outside of the potential of that type. Therefore, *creationists say evolutionists are wrong*. Each type possesses a relatively fixed set of genes, created by God, not by us. Evolutionist counter claiming that at the very least, old species eventually *splinter* into new types. More on this momentarily...

Let's now consider the possibility of materially affecting underlying genes, the theory touted by the *interventionists*.

To start, just because humans have not cracked gene creation or gene supplementation, it doesn't mean that real genetic engineering with enhanced, replacement genes can't be achieved. I believe it has been achieved, not yet by Homo Sapiens, but by others.

Replacement genetics complements both creation, the first species "type" creation factor, and evolution, the second "splintered" species creation factor. This two-factor system accepts plant and animal types created by God, while allowing types to evolve (devolve?) into splintered species, but only within the limited boundaries of their foundation type. For instance, primates remain primates.

Anything outside of species splintering requires intervention, a third species factor, and the suddenness of "Adam & Eve" anchors this three- factor system.

Primate evolution before Homo Sapiens followed various splintering paths with only minor improvements in intellect accruing over great expanses in time, as two-factor evolution works via incremental change. The human hunter/gatherers—the pottery makers—most likely resulted from this slow, two-factor splintering and nothing else. These Simple Humans acted as primates, troops led by a dominant male, no individuals allowed.

Today, our Homo Sapient gene pool certainly incorporates much of this two-factor legacy, but unlike previous primates that came about solely via splintering, Homo Sapiens received an infusion of genetic material from outside the chain. Only a three-factor infusion can explain both the vast jump in intelligence apparent in the civilization builders as compared to the older pottery makers, and the suddenness in which we came upon the scene.

GENESIS lists the descendants of Adam all the way through Noah, Abraham, and Moses. This backward chronology fixes the *creationist* date of Adam at 4,000 B.C., meaning *creationists* believe that Day 6 occurred in the year 4,000 B.C. But an *evolutionist* could drop the "Day 6" nomenclature and embrace this start date as well, based upon the following ...

The two-factor thesis begins with humans slowly evolving via the primate chain, arriving as hunter/gatherers in the very 200,000 BC timeframe that the evolutionists like, but suggests these beings as merely 'first edition" Humans, only modestly endowed intellectually, and, like other animals, stagnant in their ways, very much like elephants and Neanderthals.

Then in the 4,000 BC timeframe, outsiders selected this species for a genetic upgrade, not new switch combinations, but new foundation genes, especially in the domain of brain neurons. This 4,000 B.C. laboratory upgrade occurred in Year 4 Billion after the earth's formation (we will ponder what 4 Billion means in the *Time & the Speed of Physics* chapter, and ponder the nature of the neuron upgrade in the *Plato* chapter).

The three-factor "sudden shift" thesis goes on to claim that in 4,000 B.C., Adam & Eve, who were the first Humans given these high-powered neuron genes, became the first Homo Sapiens (meaning Humans with wisdom). Besides potent neuron implants, Homo Sapiens were also engineered to appear similar to the alien species breeding them, just as GENESIS points out: humans were made "in the likeness of God." Overall, the natural, two-factor humans "kind of" looked like the aliens in the first place; we looked "cool," but we were pretty stupid. We just needed some upgrades.

So, liking what they saw in the natural two-factor hunter/gatherer Humans, the Aliens decide to try an upgrade. And it "kind of " worked. The new but emotionally volatile Homo Sapient human suddenly possessed the many intellectual faculties we enjoy today, but this came with the aforementioned mental health drawbacks. And also, by starting from scratch, it would take many generations for Homo Sapiens to collect the significant amounts of know-how to match up with their new IQs. These three-factor Humans - the Homo Sapiens - possessed intelligence, but they knew not how to apply it. Things like Noah's Ark would be taught.

And so, upon reflection, it looks as though humankind has remained fairly ignorant ever since, and probably still is, considering the infinite potential of "know how" (touched upon in the *Plato* chapter). From the time of Adam in 4,000 B.C., a lot of wandering took place, and it took until the 2,200 B.C. timeframe for the city building to begin. The Homo Sapiens probably needed a lot of help to get started, hence the Sumerian legends of gods teaching masonry, the wheel, arithmetic, etc., described later.

And once we established the first civilizations, it appears our interlopers abandoned us, probably before the reign of the Incas. Without help, we needed another thousand years to build enough momentum to break through on our own to what we now experience as the scientific era, (or, maybe they taught us again, but indirectly). In the *Plato* chapter, the book will describe the theory that our Homo Sapiens imagination links to a greater universe of ideas, explaining our continued ascent.

Indeed, mankind accumulated most of our scientific knowledge only from the 1800's to today. Remember, we revered Ben Franklin for his simple key-on-a-kite experiment only as recently as the 1700's. Plate tectonics—the movement of the continents—only emerged in the 1960's—yes! For more on modern know-how, read Bill Bryson's book *A Short History of Nearly Everything*.

And so, humbly, ever since inception, and through this day, humankind basically plodded along under the weight of immense ignorance. Just imagine the ignorant minds of the smart three-factor Homo Sapiens in the first few thousand years of their journey.

Undoubtedly, at the onset, Homo Sapiens (on Day 6, or Year 4 billion, take your choice), had great imaginations, yet no data, yielding to fear and superstition, especially fear of the superior Aliens they then considered gods. An ignorant mind is a dangerous mind, filling in the blanks with made-up stuff.

To make matters worse, soon after Homo Sapiens arrived upon the scene, a second shoe dropped—the Nephilim—bringing more terror into the world. Can you imagine living back then?

As the book will provide, similar to the advent of Homo Sapiens, the subsequent Nephilim outbreak also occurred having nothing to do with micro-mutations. The Nephilim phenomenon instead points to undisciplined crossbreeding of these new three-factor Homo Sapiens and the other species, a vast genetic interplay. Let's consider the gravity of this...

These Aliens, though superior to us in the know-how department, were in a sense "human, all *too* human," and the bible says that some of the alien crew members suddenly pined for the improved, "fun-to-be-with" Homo Sapient girls. Boys *will* be boys. This saga will bear itself out in gory detail later when we look at the *Book of Enoch* chapter.

GENESIS says the renegade Aliens—called the Sons of God—took the girls. But as with the horse and a donkey, their respective genes did not totally match up, and so, the offspring—the Nephilim—came out as big, brutal, sex-starved, amoral psychopaths. As mentioned, the Nephilim offspring probably had recessive genes. In the future, to get a Nephilim baby, both parents would need to carry a recessive Nephilim gene and both parents would need to pass these switch options down at conception. Over time, the possibility of finding two parents able to do this would dwindle. Therefore amongst the Philistines, only Goliath and his brothers were giants, the others having standard Homo Sapient traits.

From that juncture, every bit of GENESIS deals with this horrible situation: the casting down of the rogue crew members by Michael the Archangel, the subsequent corruption of all flesh, the selection of Noah as genetically pure, the building of Noah's Ark, the Flood, the repopulation of Earth, the separation of people via language and the diaspora of Noah's grandchildren across the planet after the tower of Babel, all leading up to Abraham and then Moses. Genesis 11, below, describes Babel:

> *And the LORD said, Behold, the people is one, and they have all one language; and this they begin to do (building the tower): and now nothing will be restrained from them, which they have imagined to do.*
>
> *Go to, let **us** go down, and there confound their language, that they may not understand one another's speech. So the LORD scattered them abroad from thence upon the face of all the earth: and they left off to build the city. Therefore is the name of it called Babel.*

Hmmm... what is meant by "let **us** go down" mentioned above?

We cover Babel and the diaspora of people across the earth in the coming *Noah* chapter.

After Babel, say, 200 years post-flood, the Homo Sapiens scatter to the different ends of the earth, morphing into diverse races, cultures, and language systems *simply via natural selection gene switching*, as quickly as we breed dogs.

But what about the post-flood Nephilim? The flood ought to have destroyed both the remaining two-factor, natural-but-stupid humans plus the grotesque Nephilim, leaving the coast clear for Noah's enlightened offspring. It seems the flood eliminated the natural first-edition humans, including all those spread out across the earth, but though also destroyed by the flood, the Nephilim returned. How?

Following the diaspora after the Tower of Babel crisis, Noah's grandson Canaan settled in the Dead Sea area. It was Canaan's father Ham, who before getting onto the Ark, mistakenly took a wife assumed to be genetically pure. But she was not pure. Her gene set held Nephilim traits, and the buried, *recessive* genes would switch on down the inheritance line, so long as both parents carried Nephilim traits. The so-called post-flood Nephilim described in the bible ascended through this path.

Please note, so far, none of the chaos and terror described has anything to do with God, and one ponders that if a God wanted to rid the world of Nephilim he could have achieved this with a blink of an eye, even without a flood.

And so, the rigor-moral of the flood, followed by the failure of the flood to achieve its extermination goal ... shows the whole thing to be a botched operation performed by mortal Aliens. The folly presented by GENESIS proves with evidence that God was *not* in the middle of this. Instead, fallible alien decision-makers, the interventionists, stood at the helm of both the Adam & Eve and the Nephilim genetic debacles.

This ends the chapter on genetics. Ask yourself, *what's more likely:* Are we two-factor or three-factor beings? And, could recessive Nephilim genes still be floating around amongst the earth's eight billion Homo Sapiens?

Note: Apparently, evidence exists that other primates, like Baboons, raise dogs both as pets and to stand guard over the troop. So genetically, this "camp dog" trait clearly comes from the primate line. Likewise, the vast list of Homo Sapient intellectual faculties obviously come from elsewhere. The Baboon evidence (amazing film clips) can be found on You Tube.

CHAPTER 6

Enoch & The Book of Enoch, The Watchers

You may force me to say what you wish; you may revile me for saying what I do. But it moves. —**Galileo**

Before heading back to Moses and "the Lord," let's glean what we can from Enoch about the mortal players operating during the pre-flood era.

Enoch, the grandfather of Noah, born seven generations after Adam around 3,000 B.C., once had his account of the pre-flood era included in the Jewish bible. Enoch's account was almost lost after rabbis removed it at one point. Old Ethiopian bibles found in the 1800's still included Enoch, and these relics saved the day. Enoch, therefore, is no slouch in the annals of history, and writings attributed to him – however still intact - should not be brushed aside.

Those wishing to discredit the Enoch accounts particularly rail against Enoch's claim that he "was taken," quite often, by superior Aliens aboard their vessels, giving him a bird's eye view over the whole operation.

Enoch did not refer to these Aliens as "the Sons of God" as did others. He referred to them by function, calling them "the Watchers." Their job? To monitor the progress of the three-factor Homo Sapiens project.

Instead, some of the Watchers messed up, taking unsanctioned "shore leave" to meet Homo Sapient "babes." Sailors will be sailors! Back in the day, they called guys like this *scallywags*.

Why Enoch rose to such fame eludes me, but GENISIS says the Watchers revered him so that they finally took him for good, not to return. This meant that Enoch ascended, alive, into "heaven".

To Enoch, it probably meant that he permanently signed up for duty with the high command of the Watchers—the Admiral and his lieutenants—Michael, Uriel, Raphael, and Gabriel—whom Enoch spoke of before his disappearance.

This said, obviously Enoch and his alien friends grated against both the proponents of the Bible's old and new testaments, which insist biblical content the opinion of God, not of mortals. Hence, in order to protect entrenched institutional agendas, Enoch was never canonized (approved of) by any of the Jewish or Christian authorities. But there he is in print!

And so, the whole Nephilim phenomenon, and its non-religious implications, though sitting in plain sight within GENESIS, and reinforced by ENOCH, remains buried, never presented whole via the Book of Enoch to the layperson at temple or Sunday school. The great mystery makes one wonder "Who wrote the Book of Enoch?" as Homo Sapiens did not write in the pre-flood era. Was the following all told to Moses some 1,500 years later, *after* the events occurred?

Consider the following excerpts from the Book of Enoch, actual written accounts by the ancients we are told to ignore!

Enoch describes Semiazaz, leader of the 200 fallen angels:

> And Semjâzâ, who was their leader, said unto them: "I fear ye will not indeed agree to do this deed, and I alone shall have to pay the penalty of a great sin." And they all answered him and

said: *"Let us all swear an oath, and all bind ourselves by mutual imprecations not to abandon this plan but to do this thing."*

Then swear they all together and bound themselves by mutual imprecations upon it. And they were in all two hundred; who descended in the days of Jared on the summit of Mount Hermon, and they called it Mount Hermon, because they had sworn and bound themselves by mutual imprecations upon it.

The names of the fallen angel captains are given:

Araqiel, Râmêêl, Kokabiel, Tamiel, Ramiel, Dânêl, Chazaqiel, Baraqiel, Asael, Armaros, Batariel, Bezaliel, Ananiel, Zaqiel, Shamsiel, Satariel, Turiel, Yomiel, Sariel.

This results in the creation of the Nephilim or Anakim/Anak as described in the book:

And they became pregnant, and they bore great giants, whose height was three hundred ells: Who consumed all the acquisitions of men. And when men could no longer sustain them, the giants turned against them and devoured mankind. And they began to sin against birds, and beasts, and reptiles, and fish, and to devour one another's flesh, and drink the blood.

Enoch discusses the teaching of humans by the fallen angels:

And Azâzêl taught men to make swords, and knives, and shields, and breastplates, and made known to them the metals of the earth and the art of working them, and bracelets, and ornaments, and the use of antimony, and the beautifying of the eyelids, and all kinds of costly stones, and all colouring tinctures.

And there arose much godlessness, and they committed fornication, and they were led astray, and became corrupt in all their ways. Semjâzâ taught enchantments, and root-cuttings, Armârôs the resolving of enchantments, Barâqîjâl, taught astrology, Kôkabêl the constellations, Ezêqêêl the knowledge of the clouds, Araqiêl the signs of the earth, Shamsiêl the signs of the sun, and Sariêl the course of the moon.

Michael, Uriel, Raphael, and Gabriel appeal to "God" to judge the fallen angels. Uriel is then sent to tell Noah of the flood and what he needs to do:

Then said the Most High, the Holy and Great One spoke, and sent Uriel to the son of Lamech, and said to him: Go to Noah and tell him in my name "Hide thyself!" and reveal to him the end that is approaching: that the whole earth will be destroyed, and a deluge is about to come upon the whole earth, and will destroy all that is on it. And now instruct him that he may escape and his seed may be preserved for all the generations of the world.

God Commands Raphael to imprison Azazel:

The Lord said to Raphael: "Bind Azâzêl hand and foot, and cast him into the darkness: and make an opening in the desert, which is in Dûdâêl (God's Kettle/Crucible/Cauldron), and cast him therein. And place upon him rough and jagged rocks, and cover him with darkness, and let him abide there forever, and cover his face that he may not see light. And on the day of the great judgement he shall be cast into the fire. And heal the earth which the angels have corrupted, and proclaim the healing of the earth, that they may heal the plague, and that all the children of men may not perish through all the secret things that the Watchers have disclosed and have taught their sons. And the whole earth has been corrupted through the works that were taught by Azâzêl: to him ascribe all sin."

God gave Gabriel instructions concerning the Nephilim and the imprisonment of the fallen angels:

> *And to Gabriel said the Lord: "Proceed against the biters and the reprobates, and against the children of fornication: and destroy [the children of fornication and] the children of the Watchers from amongst men [and cause them to go forth]: send them one against the other that they may destroy each other in battle ..."*

The Lord commands Michael to bind the fallen angels:

> *And the Lord said unto Michael: "Go, bind Semjâzâ and his associates who have united themselves with women so as to have defiled themselves with them in all their uncleanness. And when their sons have slain one another, and they have seen the destruction of their beloved ones, bind them fast for seventy generations in the valleys of the earth, till the day of their judgement and of their consummation, till the judgement that is for ever and ever is consummated. In those days they shall be led off to the abyss of fire: (and) to the torment and the prison in which they shall be confined forever. And whosoever shall be condemned and destroyed will from thenceforth be bound together with them to the end of all generations."*

The Book of Enoch continues, with Enoch explaining his visits aboard the ship of the Watchers, and his various trips to different parts of the globe. No wonder the rabbis and priests voted Enoch out in compiling the books of the bible ... the grandfather of Noah knew too much!

Was all of Enoch, page after page, made up? Contrived?

Ok, let's move forward 1,500 years and get back to Moses and Joshua, to see what "the Lord" has in mind for them. *Moses Moves East* is next.

CHAPTER 7

Moses Moves East, The Assault

This chapter covers the initial extermination battles that took place in modern-day Jordan, east of the Dead Sea, while Moses still lived, before Joshua took over to lead the subsequent campaign in Canaan.

One unsettling claim of the Exodus story holds that after leaving Egypt, the Hebrews wandered for four decades before launching the attack on Canaan. The wandering seems to have lasted for 38 years, with most of the famous events happening within the first year of the Exodus, including the Red Sea and the Ten Commandments incidents. Then came the wandering of which little is written, followed by the final big year when the Hebrews left the dessert and in full-warfare mode, marched east of the Dead Sea up through Jordan, arriving north on the Jordan River to attack Jericho. As commented upon, the written detail of year one and year 40 appear very journal-like, so why did the journaling stop altogether for almost four decades?

The only things mentioned about the 38 interim years are a) Joshua's spying mission on the Canaanites, where he reported that the Hebrews appeared like grasshoppers next to the giants, and b) an early attempt by the Hebrews to attack southern Canaanite towns, which failed due to fortifications. Nevertheless, these two noted incidents frame what came next.

First, due to his resolve that the giants could be beaten, the Lord appointed Joshua the designated leader of the eventual campaign, and second, it was decided that attacking from the south was out, and that a long end-around march north to Jericho was the better strategy. Below, Joshua urging the people on:

> *Joshua son of Nun and Caleb son of Jephunneh, who were among those who had explored the land, tore their clothes and said to the entire Israelite assembly, "The land we passed through and explored is exceedingly good. If the Lord is pleased with us, he will lead us into that land, a land flowing with milk and honey, and will give it to us. Only do not rebel against the Lord. And do not be afraid of the people of the land, because we will devour them. Their protection is gone, but the Lord is with us. Do not be afraid of them."*

And so, in year 40, the Hebrews set out moving east. Yet the land east of the Dead Sea held a few proud kingdoms, and the Hebrews could not simply walk through uninvited, hence the pre-Canaan troubles with the Edomites, the Moabites, the Amorites, and the Ammonites.

But before digging into these precursor conflicts, we should dimension how big the Hebrew horde stood. After all, they had no transportation other than walking, no supply lines other than their flocks, and the women, children, and old folks traveled with the army. And so, the logistics seem impossible, one of the reasons naysayers consider the whole Exodus saga an invented mythology.

SUBJUGATED, however, keeps to its premise: what was written stands true, so we need to determine what was written about numbers to gauge reasonableness.

Before writing SUBJUGATED I had heard that two million Hebrews left Egypt, with 600,000 men of military age, and I never extrapolated these numbers out to see if they made sense. They don't! The column of marching people would be hundreds of miles long, and the flocks of animals needed to sustain the horde would reach 20 million or more. Water and sanitary measures out in the desert could not be managed. Plus, whenever Moses delivered a big speech, it seems *all* the people could gather 'round and hear his words.

Beyond these points, one must consider Hebrew population growth during their short captivity in Egypt. Only some 70 Hebrews—the descendants of Abraham—arrived in 1,700 BC and lived in the Nile Valley for 215 years. So, all told, how many people are we realistically contemplating?

Exodus never said two million. It used the word "eleph" to quantify numbers of people. This word has two usages. *Eleph* can mean a clan unit, or *eleph* can mean 1,000. One thousand *elephs* might therefore equate to 30,000 people using the clan translation (at 30 people per clan) or 1,000,000 people using the 1,000 translation. So, this *eleph* dilemma sits as the starting point of the controversy, further debated based upon the already practical matters described above.

For example, those advocating that indeed two million Hebrews left Egypt, argue that numbers like these exist in cities today—such as Manhattan, NY having two million residents—so they find it all quite reasonable. By the way, Manhattan achieves that number vertically—via skyscrapers—not via the tent city used by the Hebrews. On the other hand, on 9/11 while residing in Manhattan, I sat and watched hundreds of thousands of my fellow city dwellers choke the avenues, fleeing the city in about six hours' time, so practical, modern-day abstract arguments carry on both sides.

However, considering also that in 1,500 BC the worldwide population—including India and China—amounted to just a few million, it is unlikely that the Hebrews accounted for two million of the total. Modern-day Israel comprises only six million Jews. Overall, I side with eleph meaning "a clan unit," with the Hebrew horde sitting between 10,000 and 30,000 people. *Plus, they had the Ark!*

Let's move on to the defeat of Sihon and Og, the two Jordanian kings.

With their end-around strategy to assault Canaan by initially moving east and then north, Moses and Joshua intended to strike the Canaanites above the Dead Sea at Jericho, but they first had to contend with Sihon and Og.

Yet before getting to the cities of Sihon and Og, other kingdoms stood in the way, but these more southern people were related to the Hebrews way back from the time of Abraham. So the Lord instructed the Hebrews not to fight the Edomite and the Moabite cousins, but disclosed that the cities of Sihon and Og – which bear the names of their respective Nephilim kings - required extermination. Why?

Sihon and Og were giants, that's why! Og stood some 13 feet tall, had lived for more than 1,000 years, and upon his death by the Hebrews, they took his 16-foot bed with them and held onto it in Jerusalem for another thousand years, until Babylonia leveled Jerusalem in the 500 BC era. This Babylonian assault, by the way, was the event in which the Ark, too, was lost.

Here are some related bible passages regarding Sihon and Og:

> *Israel sent messengers to say to Sihon king of the Amorites: "Let us pass through your country. We will not turn aside into any field or vineyard, or drink water from any well. We will travel along the King's Highway until we have passed through your territory."*

> But Sihon would not let Israel pass through his territory. He mustered his entire army and marched out into the wilderness against Israel. When he reached Jahaz, he fought with Israel. Israel, however, put him to the sword and took over his land from the Arnon to the Jabbok, but only as far as the Ammonites, because their border was fortified.

Next came Og of the Ammonites:

> So the Lord our God also gave into our hands Og king of Bashan and all his army. We struck them down, leaving no survivors. At that time we took all his cities. There was not one of the sixty cities that we did not take from them—the whole region of Argob, Og's kingdom in Bashan. All these cities were fortified with high walls and with gates and bars, and there were also a great many unwalled villages. We completely destroyed them, as we had done with Sihon king of Heshbon, destroying every city—men, women and children. But all the livestock and the plunder from their cities we carried off for ourselves.

After this, the Hebrew horde sat across the Jordan river in front of Jericho, their first true "milk and honey" target, and it represented the end of the road for one of the great figures of Homo Sapient history: MOSES. According to his best friend THE LORD, Moses would not cross the Jordan into the promised land due to that ridiculous incident of the water and the rock back in the Arabian desert. Dutifully, Moses died on a mountain top on the Jordanian side of the Dead Sea.

But before leaving Moses behind, the reader should learn what some surmise about him and his 120 years on earth. No one knows for sure, but again, taking written words at face value, it appears that Moses loomed larger than even the Exodus, a titan of Egypt in his youth, as follows ...

Today, Homo Sapiens—the truly productive ones, anyway—deliver that productivity for a mere 30 years, from age 25 through 55. Moses led the Hebrews until the end at 120 years of age and launched the Exodus at age 80. Before that, he had time to do much more than modern Homo Sapiens can dream of. What might he have accomplished in his first 80 years?

Recall that he was rescued by Pharaoh's sister and raised a prince in court. Some say that "Moses" is not a name but a title meaning "presumptive Pharaoh—the next in line." Some historians connect Moses as general to Pharaoh's military campaigns farther south in the Sudan, which Egypt conquered in Moses's time. The theory goes that Moses—then called Tuta-Moses—emerged the conquering general. After the success of the campaign, he set up an administrative city to govern this vast expanse (the Nile runs 4,000 miles long), which Moses operated extremely well, so well that he outshone Pharaoh himself. This led to Moses fleeing to Media, across the Persian Gulf from Saudi Arabia, where he married a Cushite "African" woman and lived for 40 years before daring to return to Egypt at age 80, upon his first Pharaoh's death.

Only here, at age 80, does the Exodus saga begin. And when Pharaoh sent his chariots to slaughter the Hebrews at the Red Sea, Pharaoh lost his entire army. Records show that shortly thereafter, Egypt itself was conquered by counter-forces from the Sudan. I believe that Moses and his overall impact on the region was greater than we can envision. His final recorded speech at the gates of Jericho before his death follows:

> *When the Lord your God brings you into the land you are entering to possess and drives out before you many nations—the Hittites, Girgashites, Amorites, Canaanites, Perizzites, Hivites and Jebusites, seven nations larger and stronger than you— and when the Lord your God has delivered them over to you and you*

have defeated them, then you must destroy them totally. Make no treaty with them, and show them no mercy. Do not intermarry with them. Do not give your daughters to their sons or take their daughters for your sons, for they will turn your children away from following me to serve other gods, and the Lord's anger will burn against you and will quickly destroy you. This is what you are to do to them: Break down their altars, smash their sacred stones, cut down their Asherah poles and burn their idols in the fire. For you are a people holy to the Lord your God. The Lord your God has chosen you out of all the peoples on the face of the earth to be his people, his treasured possession.

The Lord did not set his affection on you and choose you because you were more numerous than other peoples, for you were the fewest of all peoples.

It is clear in Moses's final resolve that Nephilim genes required extermination.

CHAPTER 8

Time & the Speed of Physics: How Much Gets Done Per Second

Nature is relentless and unchangeable, and it is indifferent as to whether its hidden reasons are understandable to man or not. — **Galileo**

Unchangeable? We'll See.

According to this book, we Homo Sapiens exist today in our present form due to three interrelated factors: creation (energy, mass, and light formation), "organic evolution (splintered primate genetics) ... and Alien intervention (in vitro alien genetic implant). Here in Chapter 8, we'll focus on *Creation*.

Creation poses three main questions: First, who *is/was* the creator and why did the creator trigger creation? Second, how did creation physically unfold once the whole thing got rolling? Third, after the formation of things such as particles, atoms, suns and galaxies, what established life structures?

The *who and why* of the creator is, of course, unknowable, a claim solely held through belief and/or claims of revelation. And for thousands of years *how* creation unfolded also remained a mystery, but finally this functional question became fathomable once scientists framed the laws of physics and chemistry, able to envision these laws playing out within the various stages of the "Big Bang." The source of life remains hidden.

The Big Bang is very much a creationist construct. Though the deity figure launching the Big Bang remains anonymous, the idea of a *launch* by some entity sits at the heart of the Big Bang. Proponents claim that all the potential energy and matter that would become the universe exploded in one instant, super-hot, expanding outward, eventually cooling, forming the universe we see today.

Two men—and their work—"bookend" the mentioned advances in physics and chemistry. First, Isaac Newton and his insights with gravity and light in the 1700's, and second, Albert Einstein, when he envisioned $E=MC^2$ in 1905. Many, many others contributed along the way, collectively forming a unified view on *creation, time,* and *the speed of light*. This understanding of *creation, time, and the speed of light* might just represent the intellectual pinnacle of Homo Sapiens so far. Consider the following implications of Einstein's work...

According to Einstein's reasoning, as a space vessel accelerates away from its liftoff site, time elapsed on the space craft is less as compared to the expenditure of time at the liftoff site. And should the escaping vessel achieve the speed of light, time expenditure actually stops on the vessel, although it continues to flow at the launch site! Einstein imagined this via contemplation; the math equation came later. We will discuss the contemplation phenomenon in the *Plato* chapter.

And so, applying Einstein's maxim, if aliens could travel close to lightspeed, they might journey from Earth to their home planet in a week, though the Earth aged, say, 100 years during that time. Time simply indicates an abstract measurement of "how many atomic cycling (electron orbits) occurred." In the case of the Alien rocket, only one week's worth of atomic cycling occurred inside of the Alien bodies, whereas back on earth, 100 solar years of electron cycling occurred in local cells during the Aliens' absence.

Indeed, to prove this, relying upon our own humble "human" space program, we have conducted clock experiments, using two clocks.

One clock sits on the ground, the other in the space craft. When the space craft returns from its Journey, the clock that traveled shows slightly less time expended than the clock on the ground. Less atomic stuff happened in space then happened on earth, so less "time" elapsed.

Therefore, *NASA has empirically proven time relativity*, yet it remains the most difficult thing to cope with, as, day-to-day, we only experience "slow-motion time," with no one coming and going on spacecrafts to illustrate the more significant relativity dynamic. And to make the understanding of time even more difficult, consider this: time is dynamic in yet a *second* way.

The first way (just described) demonstrates that time—atomic cycles completed—moves slower as an object travels away from another object, but the second time factor claims that overall, *time—photon/electron cycle speed—has been slowing down ever since the Big Bang*. Even Einstein assumed light constant at 186,000 miles per second.

This chapter digs into the implications of time—cycle speeds—slowing ever since the Big Bang. Assuming the theory true, we will suggest how the faster atomic times of yesteryear affected getting stuff done, things such as the formation of solar systems and the evolutionary processes of living organisms.

But first, before getting into Einstein's physics, please indulge the author and consider my anecdotal, yet telling, time observation. I will use it later to make a point regarding the *productivity of time*.

In the 1960's my family moved from the New York area up to Connecticut. It seemed that other than town centers and housing developments, an endless, sprawling forest covered all of Connecticut. Walking through these forests, I encountered vast stone walls built by farmers living there before the Civil War, some 100 years prior to my explorations, mostly farmland, until recently.

Before the Civil War, 90 percent of Connecticut's land stood clear, endless farms with stone walls bordering fields. After the war, two things happened. First, easterners discovered that the Mississippi Valley offered deep soil without rocks, so those bent on farming might just as well go west... Second, those who stayed put in Connecticut took jobs in the many hundreds of riverside factories that participated in the industrial revolution. Farms faded.

And in just those 100 years from the end of the Civil War in 1865 to when I moved to Connecticut in 1964, all the forests grew back. But in 1964, the only animal life I ever saw in these great forests comprised squirrels, possums, skunks, and raccoons. One had to visit special fields at dusk to spy deer.

Then an amazing thing happened. In the subsequent 50 years a comprehensive population of animals moved in, including coyotes, bears, moose, bobcats, fisher cats, foxes, mountain lions, turkeys, geese, and wolves. In just 150 years, nature reclaimed its territory.

Experiencing the speed of reclamation, I can only imagine what might have occurred in 1,000 years, or 3,000 years, or in the 4,000 years that have passed since Noah's flood. And I ponder further, what more could have been achieved back then, assuming time more efficient, allowing much more *natural atomic advancement* in each solar year than now possible?

With the conceptual table set thus, pondering the power of time to get stuff done based upon atomic cycling speeds, let's dig deep into the physics of *atomic processes slowing down*.

We'll start with Einstein's breakthrough, $E=MC^2$, which asserts that units of Energy (E) and units of Mass (M) can be exchanged: *different forms of the same thing, akin to ice, water, and steam* (solid, liquid, gas). But based upon the *Law of Conservation*, the total of both can never be destroyed or increased (this law is soon challenged below). The C^2 parameter, though—the speed of light squared—remains the more interesting topic.

As mentioned, when Einstein envisioned his $E=MC^2$ formula, he assumed the speed of light constant at 186,000 miles per second, with E and M implicitly conserved. But how could this be, considering the extreme condition of no mass existing at the launch, *with light speed the only variable able to offset infinite energy?*

In the 100 years since Einstein's breakthrough, many scientists found different ways to measure the speed of light (C), and found it slowing down, though erratically. What can explain this erratic slowdown?

The explanation: units of mass (M) in the universe must be increasing *without* energy (E) proportionally decreasing, thus instead requiring light (C^2) to fall in order to balance off the MC^2 side of the $E=MC^2$ equation. In other words, not only can (E) and (M) be exchanged, but so can (C), the speed of light, as mass increases. Contrary to the Law of Conservation, the overall mass + energy sum can increase, as long as light slows. Sacrilegious, but if true, the speed of light suddenly comes into play as an offset to growing mass.

But how is mass growing?

Most agree that mass has grown bit-by-bit ever since the Big Bang. But they assume the proportionate reduction of energy, not light, made this happen.

But in the first moments of creation, with only energy in play, no mass yet existed—no subatomic particles, no atoms, nothing but expanding energy. In this brief setting, energy expansion (E) reached near infinite levels, with no mass (M) whatsoever to balance the equation. Instead, in place of mass (M) as offset, the speed of light (C^2) needed to approach infinite speeds to balance the extreme energy (E) levels then in play. Light back then moved at vastly greater (near infinite) speeds than today's mere 186,000 miles per second.

I consider this "creation launch moment" an *a priori* (self-evident) proof that the speed of light *need not be constant* and that it functions relative to the combined quantities of mass and energy ... not just due to objects accelerating away from each other, but also due to the quantity of mass in the universe. The fact that lab data backs this up impresses me even more than *a priori*. For more, look into Barry Setterfield on YouTube.

Ok, this speaks to the speed of light once traveling incredibly faster, but if there were no mass (M) at first, how did mass form?

Before providing an answer, please realize that since the Big Bang, mass has accumulated in vast proportions, including visible mass (galaxies), and invisible mass (tiny, preatomic particles filling every nook and cranny of the universe, including dark space and the space in which electrons travel while orbiting an atom's nucleus). Mass (M), today, is everywhere, clogging up space itself. But this still poses the question "How does energy (E) + light (C) become mass (M)?"

On one hand, we know how to turn mass into energy. Burning logs in my fireplace accomplishes this. But how is mass created from energy, the way plants grow using light photons? What exactly creates these tiny mass particles that have come to clog up every imaginable gap in the universe's fabric?

According to one construct, the generation of mass occurs when energy waves collide, effectively neutralizing speed. This causes the weightless photon particles, no longer moving at the speed of light, to matriculate into mass, and to suddenly possess weight. Something akin to water freezing, a different state of the same entity.

Let's carry the thought forward. After the Big Bang, energy waves began to collide all over the place (at first with each other), and particles with mass formed. The gravitational and electromagnetic properties inherent with mass-laden particles allowed them to pull together to form atoms.

After atoms, it was off to the races, and I mean *the races*, as light and electron particles moved so quickly back then that all of this mass generation, including the formation of galaxies, potentially happened in just a few "solar" days' time, as per GENESIS.

In the space of what we experience as one solar day, atomic processes operated *billions of times faster* than they do now, getting a lot more done. The overall efficiency of time (gauging how much gets done per second), therefore, is a function of the speed of underlying atomic processes, which always operate at the current speed of light. When light zoomed, a lot got done. As light slowed, atomic processes slowed, and less got done each year.

But the Big Bang dynamic never stops; time will get slower still. Energy waves continue to collide everywhere. Mass particles form prolifically. More and more, mass saturates space, and the speed of light decays in inverse proportion to the ever-growing level of accumulated mass. None of the components—energy (E), mass (M) or light speed (C)—stays constant. Contrary to what we once thought, the Law of Conservation applies to all three.

But as reported, changes to the speed of light appear erratic. Why? My hypothesis: light speed collapses only after enough particle build- up accumulates to tip the scale. This need for critical mass to trigger the next jump occurs elsewhere in physics.

Water, for example, can only turn into ice or steam after losing or infusing a huge build-up of calories at the zero-degree Celsius and 100-degree Celsius borders. A watched pot never boils; resistance points are how some things—including light, energy and mass—work when changing form.

We next move to the question of how did things work when light and time moved with much more productivity than they do now?

As background, one should know that in referring to light, we really refer to all forms of non-mass radiation such as x-rays, gamma- rays, radio-waves, etc., of which light waves are just one type, the only radiation waves visible to our eyes.

As with ocean waves, radiation waves have an up-and-down motion called amplitude, with each radiation class having its own amplitude shape. For example, each light color has a specific up-and-down amplitude, X-rays have yet another amplitude, radio waves yet another.

But with the ocean, water swells up and down. What about radiation, what stuff goes up and down?

After a few hundred years of scientific bickering, Einstein stepped in and sorted out that light waves consist of particles called photons, which flow up and down at the speed of light. At that speed, the photons have no mass. More so, anything traveling at the speed of light becomes both weightless and timeless. Einstein said so.

Much greater expressions of energy therefore once sat within each atom. Let's apply this boost in atomic energy to living things.

Humans have around 100 trillion cells, with each cell holding around 100 trillion atoms. That's 100 trillion cells multiplied by 100 trillion atoms, which equals "a number of atoms in one's body so vast we cannot fathom it": 10,000,000,000,000,000,000,000.

Now take these atoms and boost their atomic speed by 10 and you get one pumped-up living being able to operate at a level we can't imagine, with internal systems humming, bodies virtually unable to get sick, and slow to age.

These super beings include the first *10* generations of homo sapiens, starting with Adam through Noah, each living for 900 years. These people lived for more than 10 times our current life expectancy! That is why I, at age 65, sit here typing sluggishly. My atoms are tired.

Ok, but what about other plants and animals?

Well, if in today's slow-motion time, nature could retake Connecticut in 150 years, then a 10-speed advantage would mean that an ancient jungle could reestablish itself in 15 years, not 150. Evolutionary *natural selection* changes within species might only take a few decades, and some animals, e.g., dinosaurs, could grow to enormous size.

Following the Tower of Babel diaspora of people in 2,300 BC. the Homo Sapiens could quickly morph into the current human races as they relocated around the planet.

Time (physics) back then was very, very different. "Back then," to reiterate, still required 365 days for Earth to complete one orbit of the sun (solar time), *but at the atomic level,* 10 times more atomic stuff took place in that year than takes place nowadays (atomic productivity, or how much stuff got done per unit of time).

This leads to a few suppositions regarding Noah's flood...

The first supposition envisions the amount of pre-flood plant and animal stuff growing within this high-yield hot house. An unimaginable abundance of organic stuff explains the vast stores of coal, oil, and dinosaur bones found today, buried and compressed in mass graveyards by the flood just 4,600 years ago.

The second implication envisions the world's prolific ability to bounce back from the flood. The speed upon which the plants and animals retook the planet and then splintered into hundreds of sub- species could total many times our current expectation. The scene during GENESIS must have resembled the playback of a time-elapsed video!

The third implication is that higher atomic speeds drove higher plant metabolisms, creating higher levels of oxygen. Noah's body had fast atoms and his lungs had plenty of oxygen to fuel his cells.

Plus, fourth, being only the 10th generation, Noah's ancestral line had accumulated far fewer genetic disease mutations then we carry today. There was nothing wrong with him at all!

No wonder he lived so long...

Ok, with all of the above to set the stage, let's next dig into more detail on the flood and the post-flood time of Noah, but factor in this variable light-and-time optic.

Noah is next!

CHAPTER 9

Noah's Ark, The Flood, Babel & The Diaspora

One of the more astonishing findings of my research places Noah's flood at 2,400 BC, not even 5,000 years ago. The inductive conclusion for this date (no other explanation makes sense) is the simultaneous formation of civilizations around 2,200 BC in Mesopotamia, Egypt, India and China, all—as we will see—by the grandsons of Noah. The short timeframe of, say, 200 years between the flood and the major settlements, foots with the Hebrew claims of Genesis, with the Egyptian legends, with the Sumerian creation tablets, with the Indus Sanskrit texts, and with ancient Chinese written history. The *Evidence from Other Civilizations* chapter will present these details.

For now, by accepting 2,400 BC as the flood date, when the world's first civilizations formed via the clan migrations of Noah's grandsons, there were only a few Homo Sapiens on earth—all spread out. Since then, we grew from just 1,000 people to almost eight billion in 4,000 years (yes, we've become a problem!).

As the tiny clans spread out, they traveled with their Alien overlords, the Aliens themselves looking for new domains to possess as private kingdoms.

Because the bible is so precise in notating the generations from Adam to Noah to Abraham to Moses to David, we can place Adam & Eve at around 4,000 BC, just 6,000 years ago, leaving 1,600 years from Adam to the flood in 2,400 BC.

SUBJUGATED from the get-go has promised that everything we know happened just recently, and not as told, and this *Noah* chapter exemplifies the point.

Noah's Ark, The Flood, Babel & The Diaspora covers the geological causes of the flood itself, the ability of Noah to build an ark, the return of life on Earth, the slow growth of Homo Sapiens population after the flood, the population level at Babel 200 years post-flood in 2,200 BC, the diaspora of the various grandsons of Noah, the main settlement areas of the Nile, the Tigris Euphrates, the Indus and the Yellow River valleys, and the morphing of these settlements into races. Here is a quote from Jesus:

> *"For as were the days of Noah, so will be the coming of the Son of Man. For as in those days before the flood they were eating and drinking, marrying and giving in marriage, until the day when Noah entered the ark, and they were unaware until the flood came and swept them all away, so will be the coming of the Son of Man." (Matthew 24:37-39)*

Let's start with a condensed version of GENESIS 6-9, to see what it claimed, literally...

> *So, the Lord said, "I will wipe from the face of the earth the human race I have created—and with them the animals, the birds and the creatures **that move along the ground**—for I regret that I have made them."*
>
> *Two of every kind of bird, of every kind of animal and of every kind of creature that moves along the ground **will come to you** to be kept alive. You are to take every kind of food that is to be eaten and store it away as food for you and for them."*
>
> *Pairs of all creatures that have the breath of life in them **came to Noah** and entered the ark.*

On that day **all the springs of the great deep burst forth**, and the floodgates of the heavens were opened. And rain fell on the earth forty days and forty nights.

But God remembered Noah and all the wild animals and the livestock that were with him in the ark, and he sent a wind over the earth, and the waters receded.

At the end of the hundred and fifty days the water had gone down, **and** on the seventeenth day of the seventh month the ark came to rest on the mountains of Ararat.

The waters continued to recede until the tenth month, and **on the first day of the tenth month the tops of the mountains became visible.**

By the first day of the first month of Noah's six hundred and first year, the water had dried up from the earth. Noah then **removed the covering from the ark** and saw that the surface of the ground was dry.

By the twenty-seventh day of the second month the earth was completely dry.

After the flood **Noah lived 350 years**.

The mission of SUBJUGATED assumes these types of passages "sincere accounts." Enlightened historical constructs are needed that explain what's going on. But before we consider the explanatory constructs below, I'll offer a few comments about the ark story. Generally, my comments comprise practical musings, such as "What about sewage, and water and air supply for thousands of animals locked up in a waterproof vessel for a year?" Another point: GENISIS refers to two of each kind... Genetically this means two *dogs*, period, not two of *every dog breed*, the same for horses, sheep, etc. Rather than all of these animals, another explanation finds Noah carrying fertilized eggs of animals, supplied to him by the Alien doctors. Either way, after release from the ark, the kinds would easily "switch" (as discussed) into breeds and eventually splinter into sub-kinds. These things said, let's get to the explanatory constructs.

It starts with *Pangea*, the solo continent sitting astride the "water planet."

Before the flood, envision the earth's land masses joined together as one gigantic continent. Theorists call the single continent *Pangea*, and many accept that Pangea existed, as North and South America appear to have once fit snuggly with Europe and Africa. Chances are that at first water completely covered the earth, and Pangea formed only after a massive projectile collided with Earth, deeply rupturing the crust, creating the greatest singular "volcanic eruption" ever, probably dislodging matter resulting in the moon.

In this construct—years later—the intentional breakup of Pangea came about through the injection of anti-gravity forces into Pangea's fragile fault lines by our friends, the agitated Aliens. By accepting the existence of Pangea, we can explain multiple mysteries of Earth's past...

First, it explains why North and South America fit perfectly with their eastern counter-continents, Europe and Africa. Hey, that in and of itself is significant.

Second, it provides the likelihood that Humans co-existed with dinosaurs ... Yes! Most do not know that 90 percent of dinosaur fossils are found in the Americas. China comes in a distant second. This leaves only a scattering of remains across the other 80 percent of Earth. So, humankind, including the Simple Humans from Africa and the first Homo Sapiens from Mesopotamia, may have enjoyed seclusion in separate biospheres

... and so, with how many dinosaurs did they actually share real estate?

Third, should the Americas North and South suddenly separate from Pangea and slide westward into the vast waters of our orb, what would result? Let me help you envision what transpired. From *Geology.com*:

> *On the night of July 9, 1958, an earthquake along the Fairweather Fault in the Alaska Panhandle loosened about 40 million cubic yards (30.6 million cubic meters) of rock high above the northeastern shore of Lituya Bay. This mass of rock plunged from an altitude of approximately 3000 feet (914 meters) down into the waters of Gilbert Inlet. The impact generated a local tsunami that crashed against the southwest shoreline of Gilbert Inlet. The wave hit with such power that it swept completely over the spur of land that separates Gilbert Inlet from the main body of Lituya Bay. The wave then continued down the entire length of Lituya Bay, over La Chaussee Spit and into the Gulf of Alaska. The force of the wave removed all trees and vegetation from elevations as high as 1720 feet (524 meters) above sea level. Millions of trees were uprooted and swept away by the wave. This is the highest wave that has ever been known.*

A pile of rocks did this. Entire continents driving into the sea would cause waves tens of miles high. And the continents slid for *thousands* of miles, their momentum *incalculable* until finally they collapse against what we now call the Pacific Plate, as the Rocky and Andes mountains emerge, a vast buckling of the earth's crust. Who can deny this?

Fourth, examine North America's geological deposits. Once the continents let go, a series of slap-back waves swarmed across the sliding crust. Geologists cite six deposit layers in North America. Evolutionists believe these deposits occurred over millions of years; flood advocates explain the deposits over the course of weeks as follows:

> The most telling aspects of the six layers ties back to the fossil record, including fossil layers from aquatic animals up to Tyrannosaurus Rex. The first layers hold fossils of marine life, and these first layers stretch across both the western and eastern sides of North America, leaving an untouched corridor from New Mexico up to Montana. But each successive wave begins to close the corridor down, depositing hundreds of feet of silt, until the final sliver of America is submerged. All of the famous dinosaur deposits are found beneath this last silt deposit, as if, like Buffalo or Wildebeests, they stampeded north through the corridor looking for safety until the last. Whole herds of dinosaurs found buried together. Who can disregard this evidence?

Fifth, the landscape. And when the waters receded, great inland seas remained, temporarily trapped behind by the sediment layers. But water always seeks the lowest level, and after the flood, great quantities of water finally escaped, cutting a Grand Canyon through the landscape on its way home.

> **Side Note:** The ancient Chinese history book, the *Shu Jing*, cites that great areas of water were trapped inland and that a great engineer, Emperor Yu, living in the days of Abraham, circa 2,000 BC found ways of draining the waters without causing damage to the dry areas.

Sixth, India. Universal belief holds that during the breakup of Pangea, India swept up from lower Africa and crashed into Asia, forming the world's tallest mountains, the Himalayas.

Seventh, the aftermath. When the waters receded, many sea creatures undoubtedly survived, some plant life remained intact, but animal life? Gone. Dinosaurs? Gone. Insects? There are missing pieces, but the above explanation stands "most likely."

Assuming this "most likely" happened, given no other unified explanation yet brought forth to explain the above, what could have come next? GENESIS says that Noah planted a grapevine as his first act and gives us no further information. Too bad. Noah, though, did have three sons and 16 grandsons, and the Genesis 10, Table of Nations, chronicles that much, as follows.

The Table of Nations

This is the account of Shem, Ham and Japheth, Noah's sons, who themselves had sons after the flood. These are the clans of Noah's sons, according to their lines of descent, within their nations. From these the nations spread out over the earth after the flood — GENESIS.

The sons and grandsons, and where they settled, are listed below:

JAPHETH

Gomer — Europe
Magog — Ukraine
Madai — Iran
Javan — Greece
Tubal — Georgia
Meshech — Russia
Tiras — China/Japan

HAM

Cush — Ethiopia
Mizraim — Egypt
Phut — Libya
Canaan — Palestine

SHEM

Arphaxad—Chaldea/Hebrews
Lud—West Turkey
Aram—Syria

Either all of this was made up, or it is a "sincere account." To help support the above claims, consider evidence still present on earth:

Today, Ethiopians still call themselves Cushites (e.g. Moses's wife).

The old name for the Welsh language is Gomeraeg, from their ancestor, Gomer, whose descendants began to populate the British Isles from the mainland.

Mechech is the old name for Moscow, Russia, and one region called the Mechech Lowland still holds the original name today.

Libya is still referred to as The Land of Phut.

The languages of north and east Africa are Hamatic – after Ham – Noah's son.

Assuming a historical founding, we need to envision what became of this budding race of flood survivors. It starts with Noah living another 350 years to age 950, and his sons lasting only 400 years. After the flood, things changed, lifespans shrank, perhaps oxygen levels fell due to decreased vegetation and to new weather patterns that led to an ice age covering a third of the globe. But no matter, it all happened recently. If so, Noah still lived in Abraham's time, circa 2,000 BC. And so, the flood survivor mentioned by Gilgamesh, circa 2,200 BC makes sense.

Side Note: The Aboriginal peoples of Australia, who spoke of a global flood and how only eight people escaped in a canoe do not seem farfetched.

Nevertheless, back then, after the flood, atomic processes still hummed as compared to now, and life took off again. Assuming Noah's clan held together until Babel, as reported, and that this repopulation expanse lasted just 200 years, then how many Homo Sapiens do we have in Babel, by 2,200 BC, considering eight souls in 2,400 BC?

According to the internet growth calculators I tried, the answer comes to around 1,000. That's it. After Babel, the clans of 100-odd people split up, settling in a few river valleys in the east and in the west, with the north still covered with ice. At some point population growth exploded, but not at that point, not yet. But 700 years post flood in Moses's time, millions were likely (five to seven million), some in Mesopotamia, some along the Nile, the Indus, The Yellow and Yangtze rivers, plus smaller scatterings elsewhere. A few would make it to Australia and to the Americas.

The takeaway? We are all descendants of Noah, it only matters what grandson and what daughter-in-law bore that grandson and to where they drifted… The various locations settled by the Noah peoples are listed in GENESIS. You can look yours up, but the point remains: our common ancestor stands just 4,000 years back. Like dog breeds, Homo Sapiens are the same, just switched differently!

For more on the science of the Flood, visit *Genesis Apologetics* on YouTube.

The Babel Diaspora, Pygmies and the Little People

Possibly the best, though least factored-in evidence of the 2,200 B.C. Babel *diaspora* of Noah's grandsons ... is today's African Pygmies, who still live in equatorial jungles surrounded by the taller, very distinct Negro races. Pygmies are not small Negros.

The most illuminating aspects include Pygmy memories, genetics, language and religious beliefs, all intact from ancient times. Through mitochondrial DNA analysis (from the eggs, tracing the mother's inheritance line), they are considered one of the oldest unadulterated races on earth.

Time/History - As a marker, the Egyptian Pharaoh, Pepi I - certainly an Alien reigning soon after the diaspora from Babel - used tomb hieroglyphics to write about a Pygmy dancer transported 4,000 miles from the source of the Nile up to his Egyptian court. Pygmies apparently influenced and entertained the Egyptians for centuries, but the Pygmy people themselves - always cloistered in the jungle - were never internally disrupted. Even after Stanley – of "Doctor Livingstone I presume" - encountered the Pygmies in the A.D. 1870's, they kept their world private.

Language/Race - The Pygmies, who call themselves *The People of Ete*, claim their ancestors "white men". They possess a "Hamite" derivative language (from Noah's son Ham, and Ham's sons who colonized Africa), derived initially from the true root language of Babel which, in turn, drove many if not all of the languages on earth. For example, the Efe word for "my" is MAI, French MA, Spanish MI, Persian MIAY, German MEIN, Norse MIN. There are hundreds of other examples like this, showing that Homo Sapiens once shared a common language.

Religion - The Efe believe in an eternal God who once lived with them (i.e., their Alien escort following the diaspora). "When he lived with us – HIM, giving his orders, and us obeying HIM – we were happy, we were powerful and strong, we were the masters". In their "original sin" tradition, they say that when a woman violated the word of God at the fruit tree, God departed, introducing death to humankind.

Little People – Today's Efe Pygmies, standing at four-and-a-half feet in height, are not to be confused with the legendary three-foot humans – *The Little People* – spoken of throughout all of humankind's folk legends, though Little People and Pygmies may be a hybrid.

Legends from the time that Little People interacted with Homo Sapiens reveal the Little People night owls who squinted in broad daylight, hard workers, great implementors of earth and stone concoctions, like Stonehenge and the thousands of mounds built within the Ohio River basin, and firm in turning away from Homo Sapiens who mistreat them.

Legends talk about **Pan,** the original pre-flood home land of the Little People in the Pacific Ocean, part of **Pan**gea, off the coast of today's Ja*pan*. Were the Little People a separate Alien experiment run before the Homo Sapient model? If so, they too were saved during the flood, and were subsequently dispersed by the Aliens, just as both the animals and Noah's sons were intentionally resettled.

Note: If this Little People/Pygmy topic interests you, research the various Jean-Pierre Hallet mid-1900's works on the Pygmy tribe he lived with in the Congo, and read Susan B. Martinez's "Lost History of the Little People" – a great linguist.

And certainly become aware of the Tennessee Little People of North America.

During the 1800's in Tennessee, 75,000 human skeletons of 2 ½ to 3 feet were uncovered by farmers just west of the Cumberland gap. These were adult skeletons, with molars and ground down teeth. Many newspaper reports from the time period can still be examined.

Note: Read Fritz Zimmerman's "Encyclopedia of Ancient Giants in North America" for nineteenth-century articles on both the Tennessee Little People and the Ohio Giants.

A Time Aspect of Aliens

If the speed of physics theory is true, though 14 billion years of atomic stuff occurred since the big bang, it all happened in a relatively short period ... maybe not six days as claimed in Genesis, but in short order nonetheless.

As for advanced aliens, it does not take that much time for intelligent species to scientifically evolve. Look at us! Our alien friends might be no older than 10,000 years, providing plenty of time to develop their anti-gravity and medical advances.

They are not better than us, just older.

CHAPTER 10

Language, before 1,000 BC, A Slow Start

Every now and then a man's mind is stretched by a new idea or sensation, and never shrinks back to its former dimensions. — **Oliver Wendell Holmes**

Before delving into Joshua's conquest of (almost) 32 Canaanite kingdoms around 1,400 BC, one must understand the primitive conditions of the time, especially in the areas of language and writing.

Pre-Homo-Sapient humans (before Adam) likely used a language of *some* sort, meaning that, in part, they communicated using words, and I say "in part" as many animals use means other than words to communicate. But the exchange of specific, spoken words certainly marks a first-ever earthly breakthrough, and it could have been taking root in primitive forms for some time, even true with the Neanderthals who came before the pre-civilization humans. Neanderthals, those big dopey lugs, just may have had a small vocabulary, who knows?

As will be argued, language and writing in particular are the means to collect and store know-how, creating a platform to launch further concepts. The role of writing in establishing a knowledge warehouse operates as a prerequisite to civilization. But when Adam & Eve were advanced in IQ, making them Homo Sapiens, their offspring initially lacked the ability to write, greatly limiting their hidden potential.

Let's start this chapter by looking at language itself, realizing language is not a black-and-white phenomenon with all languages the same. Languages are systems of words, and some systems offer more efficient communication than others. The more efficient, the better the language works toward organizing thinking, allowing imagination to move current ideas forward to the next level.

That said, despite the high IQs of early Homo Sapiens, their lack of know-how and moreover, their lack of efficient written language certainly held them back, until taught communication fundamentals by their alien "caretakers" around 2,000 BC (3,000 years after Adam & Eve).

To make my language point, I *dare* propose *English* the best language so far, considering the following comparisons:

English versus Oriental—English uses an alphabet of 26 letters, a mixture of vowels and consonants that can be assembled to represent any spoken word. Many words are spelled similarly to the way spoken, though English spelling idiosyncrasies abound, easily tripping one up. But Chinese, Japanese, Korean, and Vietnamese languages are far more problematic, using discrete pictures for each word. One needs to learn and then draw a series of pictures to communicate in this manner. And in modern times, as new concepts and words race into play, the cavalcade of new Oriental pictures designed to "underwrite" scientific concepts has little hope of keeping up with the times, certainly nothing reflecting the spoken sound of the new words. Instead, they use English and mix it with picture words!

As described below, original Sumerian writing was also picture based, later copied by the Orient and by Egypt. And then somehow, alphabet systems replaced Sumerian picture methods, capable of enough words to support storytelling, a new ability just becoming available to early dignitaries such as Abraham, who lived in the Tigris-Euphrates region during the 2,000 BC written-word era.

But for some reason in the Far East and in the Americas, picture methods took root and they remain in force even until now. Overall, language locked into picture methods bears many shortcomings. English words: 400,000 (using just 26 letters)—Oriental pictures: more than one million, and the individual must learn English anyway to compete internationally.

Next, let's examine the European Romance languages that rose following the Roman Empire.

English versus Romance Languages (French, Italian, Spanish, German)—The relatively older Romance languages have two large inefficiencies. First, subjects and adjectives are gender defined, though this offers no communication value, only baggage. Does it really help to memorize a "tree" as being masculine or feminine?

Also, Romance languages have verb conjugations all spelled and pronounced differently, although some of this variation is also present in English conjugations, but not to the same degree. English: He *left*; He might have *left* earlier; He would have *left* ... Notice that "left" stays constant.

English versus German—Though both use an alphabet, German often builds new adjectives by combining old adjectives, causing long, redundant words, plus it incorporates inverse, jagged sentence structures.

English typically creates a fresh word for every new idea or description, so that the meaning is precise, and English sequencing—subject, verb, result—clues the receiver in sooner. English words: 400,000—German words 300,000 (many German words also requiring gender baggage). Consider this:

English: "We have a long way to go."

German: "Vielleicht ist unser weg noch weit," literally, "perhaps is our way yet far."

The above provides a quick look at how languages stack up now. You are free to reject what was just presented, but it still raises the question: "Who knows how language operated with the Neanderthals 200,000 years ago, with pre-civilization humans 20,000 years ago, or even with post-civilization Homo Sapiens 5,000 years ago?"

Undoubtedly, language stood relatively imperfect at all points in time, stifling communication and clarity. And for sure, one cannot easily overcome one's core language deficits. So, if spoken language has issues, then what about writing ... the function of recording complex ideas, the real foundation making intellectual advancement possible?

Written languages outside of Sumer, robust enough to record history, did not exist until around 1,000 BC. Before that, crude Egyptian hieroglyphics and Sumerian cuneiform pictures existed on a very limited scale, these percolating around 2,200 BC. (post flood). Noah did not write. Adam did not write. No one wrote, except possibly the one called Enoch—ancestor of Noah, supposedly trained by extraterrestrials. We covered him earlier.

Early writing attempts were mere precursors, mainly used to keep warehouse inventory counts, with Egyptian hieroglyphic symbols amounting to only 900 "words" and Mesopotamian cuneiform about as many. A picture of a bird, a picture of a cow, etc., all virtually useless in conveying anything of complexity.

Let's delve into the Mesopotamians, of the so-called fertile crescent, to fathom the ascent of writing.

Mesopotamian Civilization 4,000 BC (Adam) To 550 BC.

Considered the oldest civilization, the Mesopotamian historical arch consists of six major eras across 4,000 years, including Pre-flood People, and Post-flood Sumerian, Chaldean, Akkadian, Assyrian, and Babylonian eras.

These peoples spoke Akkadian and used cuneiform figures—notches in clay—to communicate in writing. At first very limited, around the noted 2,200 BC timeframe (200 years, post flood), cuneiform advanced as a workable language. Rather than using a picture of say "a noble man," a picture representing the condition "noble" surfaced, and this abstraction (separating adjectives and nouns) continued to evolve, resulting in a more fluent language. The Sumerians say they were *taught* to make this leap in approach.

To achieve this, cuneiform, once consisting of 1,000 pictures, is next reconstituted to around 600 "letters" which a writer combines to make words. Six hundred letters is a long way from the tidy 26 letters found in today's modern English, but still a big step toward efficient written communication.

Once cuneiform advanced in these ways, long-standing Akkadian folk legends, passed along until that point by word of mouth, could finally be notated, resulting in the first major work of literature known to mankind, titled *The Epic of Gilgamesh*. Noah *and* Abraham, both still living, and later Moses, *likely* inherited these stories and the underlying ability to write from whoever first instructed the Homo Sapiens.

King Gilgamesh of Sumer, who ruled circa 2,000 BC. (around the time of Abraham) had many recorded adventures within his written epic. In one, he meets an old man (Noah?), a survivor of the flood. This important literary find, of course, dovetails nicely with the Jewish flood version, which gives some credence that the flood occurred in 2,400 BC, or even later.

Some 3,400 years post flood, in the 1800's, *The Epic of Gilgamesh* was discovered on clay tablets in Uruk (Iraq). Since then, other Gilgamesh copies have been uncovered along with other stories recorded in this manner, some written around 1,800 BC, others as late as 500 BC. Written legends include the interaction of "gods" who taught humans things such as construction, irrigation, and writing. These relics speak volumes.

Also, many stone carvings still exist depicting the "gods" instructing the humans, with gods wearing what appear to be watches—perhaps timekeepers, communication vehicles, or even time-travel devices. The gods are big, the humans small. Don't discount these images.

Cuneiform writing was used by the successive empires mentioned above but dropped around 300 B.C., replaced by the Greek language once Alexander the Great conquered the Mideast. Isaac Newton postulated that the Greeks learned writing from *Cadmus*, who came out of the Mideast in the 1,000 BC timeframe (more on Isaac Newton later).

Considering that the Gilgamesh epic was written down in 1,800 B.C., and that Noah's descendants, including Abraham, came from the region in that time period, there may have been lasting cuneiform texts of Genesis and Enoch available in the time of Moses - just 500 years later in 1,500 B.C. - from which Moses crafted GENESIS. This stands another alternative to either divine revelation or "the Lord as editor" versions of GENESIS mentioned earlier.

Next in line is the Egyptian language (Coptic) which lasted from 2,200 BC to AD 1700, when Arabic ultimately replaced it.

Egyptian Civilization 2,200 BC to 1,700 AD

Coptic, a four-thousand-year language, only survives today in the Christian churches of Egypt. Complementing Coptic speech, hieroglyphic writing began later, around 2,000 BC, remaining in use until AD 400, replaced, once and for all, by Roman Latin, and then by Arabic in the post-Mohammad AD 650 era.

At that point Egypt hieroglyphic meanings were forgotten, undecipherable until the discovery of the *Rosetta Stone* in 1799 containing parallel hieroglyphic and Greek texts.

Some historians believe that the very idea of reflecting subjects in picture-writing came from Sumer, and that Egypt followed suit, creating its own hieroglyphic concoction. The same may hold true of the Far Eastern picture languages that surfaced after 1,500 BC in China's Yellow River Valley, and later in the American picture languages of the Mayan, Aztec, and Inca peoples, these lasting beyond Cortez and Pizarro until AD 1,700. Some peoples never moved beyond pictures...

But primitive language aside, the two inexplicable aspects of ancient Egypt remain: the pyramids and the shape of the Pharaoh heads— yes, their elliptical heads. To some, these two things go together as the Pharaoh heads seem alien, not primate, and hardly anyone believes that humans, just recently engaged in pottery, could suddenly have built the pyramids.

A plausible correlation is that *alien Pharaohs* directed humans to build the monuments, using the mentioned anti-gravity energy systems to move 70-ton granite stones around. No, the stones were not pulled hundreds of miles using ropes, rolling them on palm tree logs. Only a diehard "evolution or bust" type, decrying intervention, would go around explaining the construction of both Egyptian and American pyramid structures as a function of human propulsion. The same conclusions tilt true with Stonehenge and the Easter Island statues (I have personally touched both).

Even if massive human efforts could move these stones, why would people do this? Yes, today we build skyscrapers, but the human effort to do so is minor. If we did not have our machines, we simply would not attempt to build beyond our means. The ancients did not operate differently.

The elongated heads, though, are quite something. Evolutionists, rejecting aliens, claim the heads were constricted from infancy onward the way the Chinese once bound a girl's feet to keep them small. But we are not talking feet, we are talking brains, something not readily toyed with...

More so, examples of elongated heads appear in both Egypt and in the Americas. Believe what you want, but no necessary purpose, such as indicating nobility, resides in restricting and shaping the growth of the heads of one's children. Nobility has been demonstrated repeatedly through other means, especially clothing. Wear a crown, but leave the skull beneath it alone.

The point: strange stuff went on in Egypt in the post-flood era, with people using a 900-character picture language articulating little or nothing. Some postulate that engineering is mathematical and not verbal, inferring that the Egyptians might have been good at math, not words. Yet all engineering, physics, and chemistry originate with verbal concepts, next translated into mathematical expressions ... just ask Newton and Einstein. Egyptians acting alone with their narrow picture- writing and worship of the sun simply could not have fostered ancient Egypt.

Sanskrit: Let's look at India

Sanskrit is the language of ancient Indus valley peoples in India. Its written form appeared pre-1,000 BC, the same time frame in which Hebrew and Greek writing coalesced.

Sanskrit did not emerge from a picture-based system. The Indus race was Aryan, the same racial stock forming the Greek and Latin cultures in Europe, those who gravitated to letters. In India, the writing system called *Devanagari* evolved, still used today in more than 100 modern languages, including Sanskrit. Devanagari script has 47 primary characters, including 14 vowels and 33 consonants—not quite as lean as English, but approaching English efficiency. Devanagari, though, has no letter case, and spelling flows closely with pronunciation, a fairly efficient system. Regarding numbers, India later adopted the Arabic digits, including zero, in the AD 700 timeframe.

The Indus people eventually adopted Hinduism as their core religious practice, a multiple-god, multiple-class view of existence featuring reincarnation, and the reassembly of old souls in each lifetime.

Here, a modern writer, Gregory David Roberts, explains an old Sanskrit explanation of how one recognizes one's reincarnated mate:

> "The ancient Sanskrit legends speak of a destined love, a karmic connection between souls that are fated to meet and collide and enrapture one another. The legends say that the loved one is instantly recognized, because she's loved in every gesture, every expression of thought, every movement, every sound, and every mood that prays in her eyes. The legends say that we know her by her wings—the wings that only we can see—and because wanting her kills every other desire of love."

Ok. What else did these Indian ancients think? We will cover the Indian legends of aliens in the *Evidence from Other Civilizations* chapter and contemplate the many Sanskrit writings regarding *Vimana's*, the various flying saucers used by aliens back in the day. Among the things described:

> *The secret of constructing aircraft, which will not break, which cannot be cut, will not catch fire, and cannot be destroyed. The secret of making planes motionless. The secret of making planes invisible.*
>
> *The secret of hearing conversations and other sounds in enemy planes. The secret of receiving photographs of the interior of enemy planes. The secret of ascertaining the direction of enemy planes approach. The secret of making persons in enemy planes lose consciousness. The secret of destroying enemy planes.*

These guys must be taken seriously. As they shall.

Greeks... let's look at the Greeks

Similar to the Indus Valley people, the Greeks are a branch of the Aryan race, just one more offshoot of Noah. Aryans skipped the picture-based language approach and probably learned to strive for an alphabet-based system using letters to approximate the spoken word, i.e., "phonics."

The modern Greek alphabet evolved around 1,000 BC, in the same timeframe as Indian Sanskrit and Hebrew (a prior Greek alphabet was lost to historians). Other regional peoples, such as the Etruscan and Latin groups in Italy next adopted the Greek approach, and, much later, the Celtics, Russian and Germanic peoples.

Overall, this written alphabet breakthrough allowed for the recording of complex stories and ideas, building a growing base of know-how. The dates of the Trojan War stand somewhere in the 1,200 BC to 900 BC timeframe, but likely the *Iliad* and the *Odyssey*, written by Homer, came later, when Greek writing matured beyond poetic writing toward analytical prose.

The Greek philosophers who opened the door to many of mankind's advanced ontological, mathematical, political, and moral concepts came hundreds of years after Homer, in the 400 BC era after the Greeks had mastered analytical prose. We now consider these reason-oriented writings and their intellectual breakthroughs the starting points of the modern Homo Sapient trajectory leading to us, such as we are.

Ok. In those olden days, the new Homo Sapient peoples appear born with high IQs, though limited in application. But that's not all. Few of them existed, and limited population, as with limited communication, factors in understanding the ascent of the early Homo Sapiens.

Isaac Newton Footnote

Most readers of this book know who Isaac Newton was—already mentioned as a foundation physicist in the *Time* chapter—but Sir Isaac also specialized in sorting out ancient history between the dates of 1,500 B.C. and 300 B.C., essentially from Moses to Alexander the Great. Newton spent a lifetime on this, with his book *Revised History of Ancient Kingdoms* published following his death in A.D. 1727.

This amazing work endeavors to accurately date activities in the mentioned time frame by correlating the diverse figures of history across Greek, Egyptian, "Israeli," and Assyrian civilizations. If, say, an Egyptian writing claims that a certain pharaoh lived during the time of a certain Greek king, then Isaac would have a cross-footed reference to fix a date upon. The gist of his findings claims that prior to 1,000 BC, Homo Sapiens were few in number and scattered about, forming tiny, so-called cities here and there, with known historical events happening "more recently" than once assumed. Isaac, for example, calculated that the Trojan War occurred in the 900s B.C. timeframe, not in 1,200 B.C. as others believe, and that the Pyramids of Egypt are from that same era, not before.

He also claimed written language not introduced into Greece and Italy until 900 B.C.

Unfortunately, Newton could not dig further back to the flood/ civilization dates of 2,400-to-2,200 B.C. era, as the evidence needed for analytical purposes from that period only surfaced via archeological finds in the 1800's, 150 years after Isaac's death.

Writing is the keystone to advancement!

> *The increase of known truths stimulates the investigation, establishment, and growth of the arts.* —**Galileo**

And now beyond writing, we have the Internet. Consider:

> *The internet has been the most fundamental change during my lifetime and for hundreds of years. It's the biggest thing since the invention of writing.* —**Rupert Murdoch**

Now that we have established the primitive nature of pre-1,000 B.C. Humankind, let's check in with the boys, Joshua and "the Lord," operating circa 1,400 B.C.

CHAPTER 11

*Joshua, 1400 B.C.,
The Extermination of Nephilim in Canaan*

Upon the death of Moses at age 120, Joshua, probably 80 years of age himself, took charge of the Exodus project, working directly with "the Lord" to carry out their plan to exterminate the "crossbred" Nephilim giants still living in Canaan.

Back in *Moses Moves East*, we left the Hebrews traveling on the Jordanian side of the Dead Sea, quietly circumventing their distant relatives from Abraham's time, the Edomites and Moabites. But farther north, Moses's army went all out to surgically strike the two Amorite kingdoms of Sihon and Og (both Nephilim Kings), killing every man, woman, and child in the region.

Then Moses died. And now, under Joshua, we resume the story, with the Hebrews massed on the Jordan River directly across from their next target, Jericho, a big "milk & honey" city. The people of Jericho cower in fear, with reports of the feats of the Hebrew horde having spread throughout the land.

After Moses died, Joshua made an opening speech to his people, reminding those younger members of the community of the proud events transpiring since leaving Egypt 40 years ago:

> *I know that the Lord has given you this land and that a great fear of you has fallen on us, so that all who live in this country are melting in fear because of you. We have heard how the Lord dried up the water of the Red Sea for you when you came out of*

> Egypt, and what you did to Sihon and Og, the two kings of the Amorites east of the Jordan, whom you completely destroyed. When we heard of it, our hearts melted in fear and everyone's courage failed because of you, for the Lord your God is God in heaven above and on the earth below.

Next, Joshua and the Lord prepare for the assault on Jericho by formulating a plan for crossing the Jordan river:

> Early in the morning Joshua and all the Israelites set out from Shittim and went to the Jordan, where they camped before crossing over. After three days the officers went throughout the camp, giving orders to the people: "When you see the ark of the covenant of the Lord your God, and the Levitical priests carrying it, you are to move out from your positions and follow it. Then you will know which way to go, since you have never been this way before. But keep a distance of about two thousand cubits between you and the ark; do not go near it."

This "do not go near it" command proves most revealing. What force of energy did the Ark house that would soon annihilate 30 of 32 Canaan kingdoms in short order? Joshua outlines what will transpire:

> Joshua said to the Israelites, "Come here and listen to the words of the Lord your God. This is how you will know that the living God is among you and that he will certainly drive out before you the Canaanites, Hittites, Hivites, Perizzites, Girgashites, Amorites and Jebusites. See, the ark of the covenant of the Lord of all the earth will go into the Jordan ahead of you. Now then, choose twelve men from the tribes of Israel, one from each tribe. And as soon as the priests who carry the ark of the Lord—the Lord of all the earth—set foot in the Jordan, its waters flowing downstream will be cut off and stand up in a heap."

Thus the second instance—after the Red Sea—where the Ark of the Covenant projects an anti-gravity wall to stem water.

> *So, when the people broke camp to cross the Jordan, the priests carrying the ark of the covenant went ahead of them. Now the Jordan is at flood stage all during harvest. Yet as soon as the priests who carried the ark reached the Jordan and their feet touched the water's edge, the water from upstream stopped flowing. It piled up in a heap a great distance away, at a town called Adam in the vicinity of Zarethan, while the water flowing down to the Sea of the Arabah (that is, the Dead Sea) was completely cut off. So, the people crossed over opposite Jericho. The priests who carried the ark of the covenant of the Lord stopped in the middle of the Jordan and stood on dry ground, while all Israel passed by until the whole nation had completed the crossing on dry ground.*

Next a most telling statement, one claiming that the Hebrew army consisted of 40,000 men armed for battle, a number that dovetails with my previous estimate of only 10,000 to 30,000 men, women, and children having left Egypt 40 years prior.

> *Now the priests who carried the ark remained standing in the middle of the Jordan until everything the Lord had commanded Joshua was done by the people, just as Moses had directed Joshua. The people hurried over, and as soon as all of them had crossed, the ark of the Lord and the priests came to the other side while the people watched. About forty thousand armed for battle crossed over before the Lord to the plains of Jericho for war.*

This "supernatural" crossing alone reinforced the dread of all the kingdoms within Canaan.

> *Now when all the Amorite kings west of the Jordan and all the Canaanite kings along the coast heard how the Lord had dried up the Jordan before the Israelites until they had crossed over,*

their hearts melted in fear and they no longer had the courage to face the Israelites.

The assault on Jericho foretold all that would come to the subsequent 32 kingdoms. As the people of Jericho waited in terror inside the city walls, Joshua's men marched around the city with the ark, told to circle quietly. Why? After a few days of this, Joshua commanded his horde to shout and stamp, all at once. The sound waves collapsed every brick within Jericho, the city crumbled, and the Hebrews rushed in to kill any survivors. Obviously, the ark slowly destabilized the molecular cohesiveness of the brick material, allowing the sonic shock wave to serve as the final trigger. Below appear the commands of Joshua:

March around the city once with all the armed men. Do this for six days. Have seven priests carry trumpets of rams' horns in front of the ark. On the seventh day, march around the city seven times, with the priests blowing the trumpets. When you hear them sound a long blast on the trumpets, have the whole army give a loud shout; then the wall of the city will collapse and the army will go up, everyone straight in." But Joshua had commanded the army, "Do not give a war cry, do not raise your voices, do not say a word until the day I tell you to shout. Then shout".

Joshua's journal—the Book of Joshua—describes the lead-up to the collapse:

Joshua got up early the next morning and the priests took up the ark of the Lord. The seven priests carrying the seven trumpets went forward, marching before the ark of the Lord and blowing the trumpets. The armed men went ahead of them and the rear guard followed the ark of the Lord, while the trumpets kept sounding. So, on the second day they marched around the city once and returned to the camp. They did this for six days.

On the seventh day, they got up at daybreak and marched around the city seven times in the same manner, except that on that day they circled the city seven times. The seventh time around, when the priests sounded the trumpet blast, Joshua commanded the army, "Shout!". For the Lord has given you the city! The city and all that is in it are to be devoted to the Lord. All the silver and gold and the articles of bronze and iron are sacred to the Lord and must go into his treasury."

When the trumpets sounded, the army shouted, and at the sound of the trumpet, when the men gave a loud shout, the wall collapsed; so, everyone charged straight in, and they took the city. They devoted the city to the Lord and destroyed with the sword every living thing in it— men and women, young and old, cattle, sheep and donkeys.

So that's how they did it.

From Jericho, many other events transpired as the kingdoms fell, but the common denominator of the campaign bore the complete destruction of entire populations. For example, read Joshua's report on the city of Ai, which fell following Jericho:

When Israel had finished killing all the men of Ai in the fields and in the wilderness where they had chased them, and when every one of them had been put to the sword, all the Israelites returned to Ai and killed those who were in it. Twelve thousand men and women fell that day—all the people of Ai.

In many locations, the local king reigned a giant, a Nephilim byproduct of insemination by the Watchers in the time of Enoch,

1,500 years back. And now, via the army of the Exodus, these genetic bloodlines finally ended.

But the mystery remains ... why did Joshua stop at 30 kingdoms when two more remained, Jerusalem and that of the Philistines?

The Philistine territory stood south, between Canaan and Egypt, a known Nephilim society. Some 400 years later David would fight the nine-and-one-half-feet-tall Philistine Goliath, and Goliath had brothers of this same stature, so... what gives?

The overall conclusion of this chapter considers the failure of both the Flood and the Exodus to rid Earth of the Nephilim-crossbred bloodlines, showing these efforts as the flawed design of mortals, not God. But with that said, what happened to the Nephilim between the time of King David in 900 BC and today?

I propose that their recessive genes would finally run out of mating partners, but not for a long time. As presented shortly, many escaped to America, eventually killed by Mongolian tribes coming across the Alaskan land bridge.

CHAPTER 12

Evidence From Other Civilizations

In the upcoming quote, check out the battle that evolutionist Carl Sagan wages against Eric von Däniken, an alienist advocate ...

> ... *That writing as careless as von Däniken's, whose principal thesis is that our ancestors were dummies, should be so popular is a sober commentary on the credulousness and despair of our times. I hope books like his Chariots of the Gods are used in high school and college logic courses as object lessons in sloppy thinking. I know of no recent book so riddled with logical and factual errors as the work of von Däniken.*

Written by Carl Sagan, in his foreword to *The Space Gods Revealed*—a book *specifically* written to refute von Däniken

This 1960s rivalry between mainstream astronomer *Carl Sagan* and outside provocateur *Eric von Däniken* is par for the course. Sagan's technique was to get the common man amazed at the scope of the universe, using his trademark "billions and billions" nomenclature to emphasize space's magnitude. This made him a "rock star", selling books and videos, and garnishing many TV appearances where he explained the majesty of science and evolution. *Eric von Däniken's* technique was the opposite, suggesting that startling events involving aliens happened right here on earth, and rather recently. *Eric von Däniken*—the alternative alien story teller—needed to be silenced by the mainstream.

Dr. Sagan was one of many famous scientists making their mark over the prior hundred years, and to get to the top as he did, was quite an achievement. But *Eric von Däniken,* Sagan's nemesis, was the first of his kind advocating Aliens, and in his *Chariots of the Gods* book published in 1968, he threw in the kitchen sink, claiming all kinds of firm evidence of alien contact. Subsequently, some of Eric's pronouncements were found wrong or flawed, allowing people like Sagan to craft *put down messages,* and more, to use the put downs to dismiss the whole proposition of alien visitation all together.

But for all the push back von Däniken absorbed for his audacity and rushed errors, the quest to understand alien involvement in our past was launched, and thousands of von Däniken disciples rose up over the subsequent decades including great authors like David Hatcher Childress and Giorgio A. Tsoukalos. These researchers explored every scrap of evidence on earth—writings, formations, relics, carvings—and filmed their work as documentaries, broadcast both on commercial TV and YouTube. Over my lifetime, the body of work cataloguing ancient physical stuff has become vast. And so have the findings of astronomy and the efforts of UFO theorists. I urge you to dig into all of these on your own.

But note, neither Sagan nor von Daniken went as far as this book, which poses more than Alien visitation.

Besides being taught a few things by Aliens, SUBJUGATED proclaims alien intervention at the genetic level, causing both our very being while simultaneously sowing the seeds for our very demise. Carl Sagan—RIP -- would really not go for this extended proposition!

Another related topic includes UFOs. There is so much out there regarding UFOs that I will not try and catalogue or judge the evidence or lack of evidence here. Obviously SUBJUGATED starts with the premise that Aliens—able to master time and gravity—exist.

SUBJUGATED's unified explanation of Homo Sapiens "inductively" calls for, but cannot prove, alien existence. Though there are no dead alien bodies to view, thereby ending the debate, no other unified explanation exists that speaks to the genetic and historical riddles covered in this book. *Evolution* stands not the viable "riddle solver" it claims to be, for all of the reasons already given. The exaggeration of evolution's role in the sudden ascent of Homo Sapiens just 6,000 years ago, only creates more riddles. Conversely, *genetic intervention* solves historical riddles, including: our sudden ascent, our ancient myths, the earth's geography, our ability to grow knowledge, our unnatural biological characteristics, our mental unrest and our political propensities.

With that said, this chapter touches upon a few more *sincere accounts* from ancient times that reinforce SUBJUGATED's intervention theme. Let's start with the Sumerians and branch out from there.

Sumerian Creation Tablets

Sumerian tales of mankind's creation are held on seven clay tablets discovered in the late 1800's in Mesopotamia, now housed by the British Museum, London. These tablets are tedious to read, first because some of the cuneiform writing is missing, and second, due to the archaic poetic cadence of the pronouncements. Luckily many academics have devoted their lives both towards deciphering these and finding other fragments that shore up the missing bits. Some of the translated statements are given below.

As I wrote this book, people I discussed it with often wondered "why would Aliens go to the trouble of genetically producing the Homo Sapient species?" The answer: according to the Sumerians "to produce workers capable of doing the hard labor of industrial projects like the mining of raw materials" — think King Solomon's mines.

The cuneiform tablets claim that before creating Homo Sapiens, the Aliens (the gods) had colonized Earth for such purposes, and that initially Alien beings assigned to do the dirty work, objected to and rebelled against it. To fix the unrest, the upgrade of primitive humans to become Homo Sapient humans was decided upon, thereby establishing a trainable work force — think China today.

Here is the Sumerian passage concerning the initial Alien work colony.

> *When the gods like men Bore the work and suffered the toll*
> *The toil of the gods was great,*
> *The work was heavy, the distress was much.*

In order to achieve the genetic implant, one of the Aliens was sacrificed to act as donor. This Alien's genes, therefore, sit within all of us.

> *You have slaughtered a god together*
> *With his personality*
> *I have removed your heavy work*
> *I have imposed your toil on man.*
> *...*
> *In the clay, god and man*
> *Shall be bound,*
> *To a unity brought together;*
> *So that to the end of days*

The Flesh and the Soul
Which in a god have ripened –
That soul in a blood-kinship be bound.

It is interesting that other Sumerian tablets also declare the first man created in Eden, a Sumerian word which means 'flat terrain'. In the Epic of Gilgamesh, "Eden", mentioned as the garden of the gods, is located somewhere in Mesopotamia between the Tigris and Euphrates rivers, though another theory places Eden in central Africa.

The original Sumer— meaning land of the civilized kings— surfaced 500 years after Adam, around 3,500 BC. It was a collection of small "cities", each city loyal to their own sub-set of Aliens (gods), who trained the new Homo Sapiens in the ways of civilization, mainly agriculture and craftmanship. It was in this era of interactive coexistence between Alien overlords and fledging Homo Sapiens that the illicit cross breeding occurred resulting in the Nephilim. This is also when Enoch, Noah's grandfather, lived.

The Greeks

The Greek classics—the *Iliad* and the *Odyssey*—plus the earlier *Argonauts* saga (circa 1,500 B.C.), contain ongoing references to the Greek gods. Most of the readers of SUBJUGATED have read these accounts and probably assumed them exotic fantasies. To put these tales in proper context, be reminded that there are two Greek eras, the "modern" one from Socrates' birth around 480 BC to Alexander the Greats death in 323 BC, and a much earlier one from 1,500 BC to 1,200 B.C. This older period claims Hercules, Jason, Achilles and Odysseus as leading characters, all battling it out with various gods and demi-gods. In this *Mycenae* era, Greece had populated Sicily and the coast of Turkey, where it fought with its Trojan cousins around 1,250 B.C. (Newton says 900 B.C.).

This early Greek civilization had a writing system since lost, replaced by the Greek system that morphed into the various languages of Europe. The mentioned sagas were written down in modern Greek 600-to-800 years after they occurred, so there is room for error, to say the least.

But consider this. The ancient Greek tales of giants and gods parallel all the others of that era. Just as the Sumerians had specific gods (aliens) dwelling in each city, Greece may have had a similar interaction with alien overlords, including cross breeding—as Achilles is said to have come from a God and a human mother.

The Olympian aliens operated like this for 1,000 years. Overall, I put the ancient Greek sagas high on the "most likely" scale for sincere, true accounts.

Chinese Writings

China was only colonized by Noah's descendant *Tiras* after the diaspora of 2,300 B.C., and Aliens appeared to have led Homo Sapiens to China, probably to set up shop elsewhere on the planet. Here are some of the Chinese *sincere accounts*.

The *Yellow Emperor*, considered the father of Chinese civilization, a demi-god (something greater than man, but less than god—sounds like an Alien), taught the hunter gathering peoples many things. Historians place the Yellow Emperor at around 2,200 B.C., 200 years post flood. In the ancient book of *Huangdi Sijing, or the Yellow Emperor's Four Classics (just archeologically discovered in 1973)*, the Yellow Emperor's lessons are listed, including: building shelters, taming animals, the five grains, carts, boats, clothing, music, mathematics and medicine. These are echoed in another ancient Chinese book called, *Classic of Mountains and Sea*, both writings *sincere accounts*. I surmise that the Yellow Emperor taught acupuncture, as it seems an unlikely art uncovered by trial and error.

And like the Indian Indus River accounts of warfare amongst the "gods" using advanced technology (coming up next), the Yellow Emperor too engaged in warfare with other mighty opponents. He conquered all enemies but *Chi You*, who had thwarted the Yellow Emperor in nine straight battles. Finally, a woman goddess, the *Enigmatic Lady*, came to the rescue, delivering weaponry that caused gigantic fogs and pounding rainstorms. One weapon she brought triggered by the pounding of eighty battle drums brought down enemies of the Yellow Emperor, similar to Joshua's use of "the shout" to level Jericho after it being destabilized by the Ark.

Finally, like Enoch, the Yellow Emperor, when 117 years old, ascends to heaven in a "dragon" that housed 70 of his closest advocates. As said, these are sincere accounts.

After the Yellow Emperor's time, further Chinese *sincere accounts* continued. Here is just one of many as told by Chinese witnesses.

This abduction account comes from a manuscript called the Da Li Gu Yi Shu Chao, dated 1528 A.D.

> On the seventh year of Jia Jing, of the summer of the fifth month and day three, there was a "guest star" which appeared, flying from the southeast towards the northwest, bright and shaped like a giant wheel, sometimes hovering high and low, and sometimes moving and stopping, and it was witnessed by more than a thousand people.
>
> At midnight, it appeared again, returning along northwest at Lu Tao village in Diang Chang Mountain and descending in the village. There was a stonemason by the name of He Geng

in the village, working at the foot of the mountain, and seeing the light from the scaffoldings. There was an object shaped like a grinding wheel, yet big as a house, having all kinds of colorful illumination, which resembled men, but not quite men. They captured He Geng and brought him into the structure of blinding light.

Within, they extracted the heart from He Geng to observe, yet he was unhurt, and not bleeding. They spoke but were unintelligible. After which He Geng lost consciousness. In his dream, he was in a celestial realm, that was not of mortal, in view of the cosmos, of an empty void, with no familiar dwellings. There were people but not resembling men, like humanoids, with three eyes, and all of them, did not wear human-like costumes or spoke human-like languages. As he observed, it just got very confusing.

When he woke, he was at the work site, and when he returned home, he realized one year had passed, and family members thought he had been devoured by beasts. They came and observed him and found a red scar on his chest, which bore no pain.

This observer had no agenda, no sci-fi movies to egg him on, and no scientific framework to guide him, and yet he reported this in such a straight-forward manner.

Moving on to India ...

India

From the Indus Valley, in the Sanskrit Samaraanganasutraadhaara it is written:

Strong and durable must the body of the Vimana be made, like a great flying bird of light material. Inside one must put the mercury engine with its iron heating apparatus underneath. By means of the power latent in the mercury which sets the driving whirlwind in motion, a man sitting inside may travel a great distance in the sky. The movements of the Vimana are such that it can vertically ascend, vertically descend, move slanting forwards and backwards. With the help of the machines human beings can fly in the air and heavenly beings can come down to earth.

This sincere account of Vimanas—flying ships—says it all. Who would make this up? How could someone in 1,500 BC make it up without witnessing it?

From the Indus River Valley, in the Mahabharata, alien warfare is described.

Gurkha flying in his swift and powerful Vimana hurled against the three cities of the Vrishis and Andhakas a single projectile charged with all the power of the Universe. An incandescent column of smoke and fire, as brilliant as ten thousand suns, rose in all its splendor. It was the unknown weapon, the Iron Thunderbolt, a gigantic messenger of death which reduced to ashes the entire race of the Vrishnis and Andhakas.

This sounds like another Sodom and Gomorra nuclear incident. Is it all made up?

By the way, while in Afghanistan, *Alexander the Great* purportedly gave a description of "dozens of silver disk-like objects" entering and leaving the Jaxartes River in 337 BC. Alexander, so the story goes, then became obsessed with the craft and spent many hours in a primitive diving bell searching for them.

Overachiever!

Now to Mesopotamia ...

Mesopotamia

In Babylonia—central Mesopotamia—from the Hakatha Laws it states:

> *The privilege of operating a flying machine is great. The knowledge of flight is among the most ancient of our inheritances. A gift from 'those from upon high'. We received it from them as a means of saving many lives.*

From Chaldea—southern Mesopotamia - the "Sifrala" contains over one hundred pages of technical details on building a flying machine. It contains words which translate as graphite rod, copper coils, crystal indicator, vibrating spheres, stable angles, etc.

Then Egypt ...

Egypt

In Egypt, From the Zep Tepi saga (the First Time saga), When Gods Ruled the Nile:

> *It was a golden age, during which the waters of the abyss receded, the primordial darkness was banished, and humanity, emerging into the light, was offered the gifts of civilization.*

The Egyptians also referred to intermediaries between gods and men—the Urshu—a category of lesser divinities whose title meant *'the Watchers'*.

And in the America's ...

The Mayans

As described in the *Language* chapter, the Mayans - a two-thousand-year civilization - from 1,000 B.C. to 1,000 A.D. - used hieroglyphics and did not have a phonics-based system to record their detailed thoughts. Still, the Mayans offer four types of evidence for Alien interaction.

First, many carved figures show elongated skulls and large almond-shaped eyes.

Second, for a hieroglyphics-based people, they somehow possessed great astronomical know-how of the planets—*even the invisible ones*— and the pace of their respective revolutions around the sun, leading to an accurate calendar projecting solstices out to the year 2012. Go ahead and try it!

Third, their pyramids, which, regardless of the many far-fetched explanations claiming hordes of laborers built them, contained rare elements like mica and mercury, used in electrical and signaling contraptions.

Fourth, the *Popol Vuh*, a history dictated to Spanish missionaries in the 1500's by Guatemalan Mayans, portrays the Mayan *Genesis* rendition, example:

Men came from the stars, knowing everything, and they examined the four corners of the sky and the Earth's round surface.

This body of evidence is so compelling that government officials in Mexico claim alien intervention the most likely explanation. There are over 50 Maya and Aztec pyramids in central America, and the Aztecs told Cortez they did not build them, they just occupied them.

In 2002, I went south to Belize and took a two-hour dirt-road trip through the jungle to visit an un-excavated Mayan city. Only one side of the city's giant pyramid was cleared, the jungle still growing on the other three sides. Climbing to the top, I saw bulging lumps in the jungle five miles in all directions. These were the other covered buildings of a once-thriving city, miles in diameter.

When the Aliens were amongst them, the Maya thrived. After 1,000 A.D. with no further Alien contact, *millions* of Mayan people suddenly vanished. This is one of the great mysteries of Homo Sapient history. Legends of warfare amongst Mayan gods (kings) amongst each other, might explain the sudden death of 20 million people.

On Easter Island

In 1991 when I visited, only one dirt road circled the island. I borrowed an off-road Wrangler and literally toured the whole island in cross country fashion to view the volcanoes and the giant statues, the Moai. Could locals have carved gigantic blocks of stone from the volcano beds, sculpted them, dragged them, and stood them up throughout the island? Maybe, but why? Why devote a society's skimpy resources to something like this?

Today, yes, as we have trucks and cranes that match our aspirations, but then, manually? I doubt it. I surmise anti-gravity commonplace in the Alien world. We simply haven't caught up yet (though funding for anti-gravity research has been provided by multiple governments since World War II).

And so, as I stood in front of the 1,000 Moai dispersed throughout Easter Island, and stared up at those almond-eyed, other-worldly monstrosities, my gut said "Aliens and anti-gravity".

Stonehenge

I have visited Stonehenge multiple times, as well as experiencing many other stone formations in England, Scotland, Ireland and Karnak, France. Stonehenge is different. In comparison, all the other formations are dwarfed in scale, able to be built by the people of the time using their technology—physical hauling. But the Stonehenge blue stone components are 30 feet high, weighing 25 tons each, mined from a quarry 20 miles north. These, like the Egyptian pyramids, are positioned so precisely as to align with various planetary cycles. Quite simply, Alien participation is the more likely explanation for a project happening post-flood around 2,200 BC.

Stonehenge may not represent "beyond a reasonable doubt" proof of alien influence, but alien participation rings more plausible when staring at 25 ton rocks.

Peru - The Paracas Skulls - "Hiding in plain sight"

In the 1920's, elongated skulls with intact DNA were discovered in Paracas, Peru – the Paracas skulls. Over time, six findings surfaced: 1) mitochondria DNA from the skulls (inherited from one's mother), is neither human nor primate, 2) the skulls are 30% larger than human skulls, 3) rather than the multiple skull plates humans carry, the Paracus forehead plate connects to a single skull encasement. 4) The skulls carry wavy red hair not found in other native Peruvians. 5) The skulls are only 3,000 years old, and 6) similar DNA has been uncovered within elongated skulls found in the Black Sea region.

Apparently, no one in mainstream science is digging into this collection of skulls held at the National Museum of Archaeology, Anthropology and History in Lima, Peru. Look these up on the internet.

Summary

There are many recorded descriptions from ancient times that speak to these kinds of experiences, and so one can only assume that the world of mainstream academia actually works in denial of what they are directly told by ancient peoples. Voices from the past contradict evolution's narrative of evolution-alone causing Homo Sapiens. Mainstream academics label alien advocates "conspiracy theorists", but it is they who run a conspiracy against written and relic-sourced history.

One should ask, am I to reject every ancient sincere account and stick to evolution as the total answer, or should I solve ancient riddles with more likely explanations, the explanations described in writing by the historic witnesses?

Ok, the above listing gives you an idea. But there is more coming out of America.

CHAPTER 13

Renegade Primate/Aliens
The Bigfoot Species

Having just covered ancient writings that focused on Homo Sapiens, we should not make the mistake of believing ourselves the only version of Primate/Alien genetics. In the next chapters we will visit with three of our relatives: Bigfoot, The Little People, and the Ohio Valley Giants.

We start with the Bigfoot race.

Today, one assumes the African gorillas the only remaining large primates other than ourselves. But the fossil record throughout Asia shows that species, like Gigantopithecus, once inhabited the vast Asian landscapes not yet populated by Homo Sapiens. It is postulated that both these great apes and The Neanderthals were terminated by Homo Sapiens.

But before their demise, Gigantopithecus may likely have been the baseline species that led to today's mysterious Bigfoot primate, explaining how Bigfoots communicate, and their extreme, almost magical, illusive nature.

Based upon sound recordings, like dolphins and whales, Bigfoots communicate, not with words, but through frequency variations, extending into high pitched registers. To hear a Bigfoot – sounding like a siren – visit BigFootBase.com. Link below:

https://bigfootbase.com/bigfoot-evidence/sounds/#:~:text=In%20 1994%20Finding%20Bigfoot's%20Matt%20Moneymaker%20 recorded%20a,used%20to%20this%20day%20for%20"Bigfoot%20 call%20blasting".

Similar to when Aliens upgraded primitive Humans into Homo Sapiens, foundation Gigantopithecus embryos were likely infused with alien neurons, but this time with a different blend. The neuron genes included an alien ability to slightly shift time, a fourth dimension.

Today, us Homo Sapiens navigate in just three dimensions – up, down and sideways - and cannot accelerate or rewind our movements in time like digital TVs. And though Homo Sapiens enjoy links to the world of ideas, and to other dimensions, such as those of intuition and ESP, we are fixed in time.

Sasquatch, the first Bigfoot, would not be so encumbered.

Why? Energy operates differently than matter. Energy particles, like electrons and light photons, have no weight. Each energy packet exists as a spread-out wave – like ripples in a pond. This is why one cannot pin point the location of an electron. Potentially it resides simultaneously in many locations across the span of the wave form. Today, we call this kind of thinking *quantum physics* – the physics of energy and time.

And though Homo Sapiens only began to explore quantum physics in the days of Einstein, our alien parents have lived by it in perpetuity. And not just in designing their time/space travel apparatuses, able to avoid missile attacks by "ducking into time", but also in operating their own organic selves.

By slightly shifting energy wave forms within, those with this ability can shimmy out of current time into an adjacent time cell.

To someone stuck in time – like ourselves - the Bigfoot suddenly disappears.

The theory goes, that the Yellow Emperor of China (the Alien who escorted Tiras and the Homo Sapiens out of Babel to China) decided to try this faculty out on the Gigantopithecus primates. Accordingly, male and female Gigantopithecus embryos were manipulated. Out of this came the first enlightened Bigfoot male and, the first female ... the Bigfoot versions of Adam and Eve.

And it worked, except for one problem. Once the Bigfoot offspring mastered this "time shimmying" ability, they decided to use it to hide from their overlords, an unintended consequence of bestowing the ability within the primate line. What is more, the hybrid Bigfoot species also inherited the independent streak that aliens are known for. Yes, libertarian Bigfoots were afoot!

And so, as the brood multiplied, like all liberty lovers, the Bigfoots wanted to separate from both the Yellow Emperor and the Emperor's Homo Sapient slaves.

As the escaped plan unfolded, some fled into the Himalaya mountains – becoming today's abominable snowmen. But most of the Bigfoot clan crossed the Asia/Alaska land bridge into North America.

Here they live today, known as Bigfoots, though American Indian legend calls them Sasquatches.

At first, the small clan settles in the Pacific Northwest, where they easily multiply and spread out across the continent. Existing alone for centuries, eventually American Indians coming in from Mongolia, moving east from the Pacific coast, and later Europeans moving west from the Atlantic coast, encroach Bigfoot's world.

As mentioned, recently Bigfoot voices have been recorded - jesting with those who dare invade their wilderness domains, with footprints sometimes found. But it is their ability to disappear in time with that slight energy shift which keeps them isolated, safe from the Homo Sapient race.

Through biological stealth, Bigfoots can live in many North American regions. Tempestuous creatures who can lash out at and intimidate invaders, and even take Homo Sapient wives, revered as preservers of nature, and sometimes connected to UFO sightings, ... they, like Homo Sapiens, accumulate knowledge and history which they employ for their well-being in their own way.

Today, their instinct for danger is so refined that by using time shifts they can evade bullets the way their alien ancestors evaded missiles. Yet, a website called SasquatchChronicles.com lists 35 reported Bigfoot killings between A.D. 1800 and now. Link:

https://sasquatchchronicles.com/forums/topic/list-of-bigfoot-shootings-in-chronological-order/

If all this is not sufficiently bizarre, there have been many reports of UFO crafts taking Bigfoots on board. To look into this, visit MysteriousUniverse.org. Link:

https://mysteriousuniverse.org/2021/05/bizarre-cases-of-bigfoot-and-ufos/

These are not kidnappings but what appear to be scheduled meetings. If Bigfoots are part Alien, then why couldn't they have a particular interaction with modern Aliens, especially if both the Bigfoot and Alien beings share quantum physic attributes?

Don't forget, like the Sun, the Planets and all the Stars revolving around Earth, Homo Sapiens crave being at the center, the sole story. Even when considering if Aliens exist on Earth, this possibility can only pertain to us, the Homo Sapient.

CHAPTER 14

Renegade Primate/Aliens The Little People

Where to start?

First off, the *Little People* were not some sort of Homo Sapient mutation – like dwarfs with mis-proportioned heads – they were a separate, elegant race trying to survive alongside the Homo Sapiens. At some point, they came to America. Consider their plight according to the ancients:

Pliny of Rome's *Natural History*

> "In the most outlying mountain region of Sythia we are told of the Pygmae who do not exceed twenty-seven inches (2 ½ feet) in height. This tribe, Homer of the Iliad has also recorded as being beset by cranes. It is reported that in springtime their entire band, mounted on the backs of rams and she-goats and armed with arrows, goes in a body down to the sea and eats the cranes' eggs and chickens, and that this outing occupies three months."

Aristotle's *History of Animals*

> These birds [the cranes] migrate from the steppes of Scythia to the marshlands south of Egypt where the Nile has its source. And the story is not fabulous. There is in reality a race of dwarfish men, and the horses are little in proportion, and the men live in caves underground.

The tiny beings mentioned are not to be confused with today's Pygmies of central Africa who, at 4 & 1/2 feet, inherited the "Pygmy" moniker from the original pygmies-of-legend who roamed the earth thousands of years ago.

Folk law abounds about this lost race inhabiting earth before the spread of Homo Sapiens. The "Little People" as called, were everywhere, tiny human-looking, red-haired beings just two-to-three feet tall, living in caves, mainly vegetarian, with squinty eyes, generally operating at night, willing to help, but quick to find fault, and often playing the role of tricksters. This undisputed description of them is universal, and so we must not ponder their existence, but instead explain where they came from and how and if they ended.

Legends insist that they lived before the Homo Sapiens, making the Little People a first edition Alien experiment – primates upgraded into a usable species of underground mine workers. And though different from the second edition *Homo Sapiens*, genetically, *Pygmies* were close enough to cross breed with us, the larger version, hence the modern day Pygmies of the Congo jungle.

But what of the original 3-foot species? Thousands of folk legends from every culture say the Little People slowly retreated to find remote virgin pockets to survive in. As a species, they ultimately clung to just a few places – such as Indonesia and the Americas. Until then, they overlapped with Homo Sapiens, sometimes cooperatively, sometimes via interbreeding, sometimes as slaves and sometimes by being slaughtered.

But do not overlook that both the Little People and the Homo Sapient primates shared an important link; they were both part Alien.

Still, as interesting as the Little People "genetic design" turned out, ultimately they were not what was hoped for by their alien scientists. Little People hated the sun, they lived underground, and they remained obstinate, timid primates, overly dependent upon their environment, not showing enough of that "alien spunk".

Oh well, we'll do better next time with our improved concoction: the aggressive Homo Sapiens, who will want to dominate nature.

Besides their shout out in the Iliad, it also was written that around 1,400 B.C., Little People in Libya climbed onto a sleeping Heracles trying to "tie him down", though the makeshift bonds were easily discarded once the hero awoke. What pests they were!

As well, Saint Augustine of A.D. 400 – the super intellect of Christianity – who pondered the world's disparate human forms in his City of God book, by asking *"Whether Certain Monstrous Races of Men Are Derived From the Stock of Adam or Noah's Sons"*, never contemplated that some of these known aberrant beings were simply genetically produced either by alien design or by random cross breeding of alien-designed beings. What a mess!

And here is the big shocker: Certainly Noah and his sons were not the only ones saved from the flood. Many Little People who originally resided in "Pan" - a landmass part of **Pan**gea east of Ja*pan (notice the "pan")* – were saved when Pan sunk during the flood.

Once saved, the Little People - being vegetarians who could immediately survive without meat - were quickly re-instated by the aliens upon the rapidly recovering earth. Conversely, Noah's offspring had no choice but to give the animal kingdom time to re-establish itself, needing to wait 200 years beyond Babel for Homo Sapiens to spread out to the Earth's corners.

Because Homer's *Iliad* – that mentions the Little People - places the Trojan War occurring sometime around 1,200 B.C., it must be after this time, say 1,000 B.C., that, in earnest and fear, the Little People race started its defensive migration out of Eurasia, ultimately depositing themselves in South East Asia and America, and particularly – of all places - in Tennessee. Yes, they could have walked to Malaysia, but the question is, how did they get to Tennessee and how did they end there?

You may be asking for proof of this Tennessee story line.

In 1875, the *New York Times* printed an extensive article reporting that since 1820 thousands of shallow graves with "little people" had been dug up by farming ploughs near Sparta Tennessee, right beyond the Cumberland gap. First considered the graves of children, scientists from the Smithsonian and elsewhere eventually confirmed them small-bodied adults with mature, ground-down molars. But due to shallow graves and scientific neglect, the remains were plowed under.

An estimate of 75,000 Pygmy graves were destroyed by local Tennessee farmers. Yet, throughout the 20th century, in both North Carolina and Tennessee, many underground dirt tunnels 4-feet in height leading to underground chambers were uncovered -their humble abodes.

Fortunately, in modern times, another find was made. Enter: *Homo floresiensis* - the real-life "Hobbits" of Indonesia. Found in A.D. 2,000 preserved in a cave on an isolated island, this ancient race was discovered with intact skulls and stone tools, also 2-to-3 feet in stature, deemed "pre-human" and called Hobbits by some and *Homo floresiensis* by anthropologists who - as is the want of today's geologists and anthropologists - claimed them a million years old.

Nonetheless, somehow, the Indonesian branch of tiny travelers must have gotten there, even if by boat.

And let one not forget that Little People abound in Irish, Welsh and Scottish legends, who for hundreds of years lived cooperatively with the Celts until the Celtic crossover to Christianity took place in the A.D. 500 era. After that, the Little People were hunted down, not just in the British Isles, but throughout all of Europe out to the Ural Mountains of Russia.

Yet they may still survive. In 1820, the official census of Kauai Hawaii – where I visited - listed 65 "Menehune", 3-foot Little People, the descendants of Pan, as part of the official population, who according to Kauai legend, lived there in the Nepali coast valleys (which I visited in 1991) even before the Polynesians.

And so, one needs to assemble a more likely explanation for all of this besides it being fodder for U.K. fantasy films or it being used as invented "descent of man" evidence cited by the many enthusiasts of Darwinian evolution.

Back in 1,000 B.C., the Little People still had many relocation choices. The Celtics of the British Isles would not arrive for many centuries, the Orientals from Asia had not reached the thousands of islands of Indonesia, and the Mongol tribes coming across the land bridge into North America would not move east from the Pacific Coast for a thousand years or more. Instead these wandering Asian immigrants drifted south into Central and South America. In 1,000 B.C., the Little People were still safe.

Later, as *Mongolian-American* tribes finally made contact with these American renegades, they gathered stories like the following about the Little People:

> *The Mohegans describe small people who lived below Mohegan Hill in Connecticut. They were not to be spoken about during the summer when they were active, and not to be stared at; otherwise, they would freeze you and steal your things. In*

return for the food and respect, they taught how to grow corn and use healing plants.

The Eskasoni in Canada say that little people lived on a hill in Nova Scotia. Children were told not to go near it, lest they be stolen.

The Shoshone tribe in the Rocky Mountains tell of little people who used bows and poisoned arrows to keep trespassers away.

The Choctaw called them Kwanikosha, who supposedly kidnapped boys to test them and figure out their nature.

The Cherokee tribe believed in three different types of Little People: the Laurels, the Rocks, and the Dogwoods. They ranged from being good and helpful to being purely malicious.

The question becomes, did the American Little People emigrate from Ireland or from Indonesia? Considering that they settled near the Cumberland Gap, a guess says they came across the Atlantic, found the North American eastern seaboard, marched inland through the Gap and hid amongst the Allegheny mountains.

Considering their size, and wondering how they could cross a vast ocean, one can also guess that they walked across the Alaska land bridge and made their way east across an empty American land not yet populated by dangerous Mongolian-Americans.

No matter how achieved, any Little People migration path represents an extraordinary epic showing immense skill and grit.

Once in Tennessee, finally in a secure isolation, they would live for 2,000 years before the western Cherokee moved east to greet them in the A.D. 1,200 time frame. But there may be another path-to-Tennessee.

As will be seen in the subsequent Ohio Giants' research, during the just-mentioned 2,000 year period, the 3-foot Tennessee Little People somehow lived in peace adjacent to the Ohio moundbuilder Giants, who reached 7-to-9 feet in height.

Considering that global legends of the Little People claim them hyper-productive builders, to survive, the Little People obviously had some meaningful alliance with the Giants, probably as the nighttime labor force constructing the thousands of earth works built from the Great Lakes down through the Ohio and Mississippi river valleys. A labor exchange for food arrangement.

Which leads to this likely explanation. When the Nephilim Giants escaped Israel and later abandoned their British Isle outpost, they brought some of the Little People with them. In America, Little People and Giants coexisted until the Giants were rubbed out by the Iroquois, and the Cherokees arrived to create new cooperative alliances with the Little People. Cherokee folk law describes the Little People as follows.

> Said to remain invisible most of the time, watching humans from afar, inhabiting the most remote mountain peaks and darkest caves. Known to appear to the Cherokee during times of need, fiercely protective of the tribe, and would rally together with forces of invisible warriors to drive away enemies.
>
> They constructed elaborate townhouses underground or within mountains. Humans who were lost or injured often told of being brought to these subterranean homes to be nursed back to health, and some Cherokee were said to even go off to live with them permanently.
>
> The Little People were capable of doing good deeds for people who treated them with respect. However, to look upon one was bad luck, potentially resulting in premature

death. Usually, those who encountered the Little People were warned by them not to tell others. It is also considered bad luck to even speak of the Little People.

When humans built homes near the Little People, it was important to leave food for them and not to block any of their paths. If the little beings were pleased, they did chores at night, like plowing fields and harvesting crops, as the Little People once did in Ireland. Sometimes the people in the house heard the work being done, but knew not to look outside.

When the Cherokees were driven out of the Cumberland area in the 1830s - during the dreadful *Trail of Tears* clearances – supposedly a few Little People families went with them, but most were left behind. After this, no further mention of the American Little People surfaced.

Yet according to Cherokee legend, the Little People, like Sasquatch, have the ability to duck into adjacent time cells. Possibly they survive, hidden away in their underground biospheres.

CHAPTER 15

Renegade Primate/Aliens The Ohio Giants

Finally, the just mentioned Ohio Giants ...

Moses, Joshua and their Exodus exploits took place circa 1,400 B.C., with the Hebrew army attempting to kill every crossbred Nephilim man, woman and child living in Jordan and Israel ... including King Og, the 13-foor giant, and all others across 32 kingdoms. How many escaped?

1,400 B.C. was just 1,000 years after the separation of Noah's grandsons out of Babel. In 1,400 B.C., few people lived on earth, possibly only a few hundred thousand, and so there were plenty of places where one could hide from the aggressive Homo Sapiens.

Also at the time, a retreating ice age still held sea levels down, and vast, open shore lines served as pathways allowing one to quickly move from place to place. More, in 1,400 B.C., the British Isles were connected to mainland Europe by a valley called Doggerland. The sea waters would only rise up over the next 1,000 years creating the islands we know today.

And so, back then, one could walk to Ireland from the Mideast along the open coast, unperturbed by others.

Stonehenge, said to be built by the "Beaker People" circa 2,200 B.C., is the world's most famous circular soil and rock "henge". The Beaker People were a branch of the Little People, just explained above. Recall, that the Little People specialized in mining and earth-oriented work, were actually bred to do so by aliens before the start of Homo Sapiens in 4,000 B.C. timeframe. Later, henge building became the passion of the Britannic Little People.

Since the flood of 2,400 B.C., the Beaker's, therefore, were able to cultivate the British Isles their way, and across many centuries they built henges – temples to the sun – throughout the reaches of Beaker territory. But their isolation ended when this race of 3-footers suddenly met a race of 8-footers walking up their beach! The Nephilim had arrived.

But the two races find common ground. Nephilim giants appreciate the work ethic of the Little People, and the Little People appreciate the higher civilization benefits of agriculture and sea travel brought in from Mesopotamia. The two races live in harmony in Britannia for six hundred years from 1,400 B.C. up until the 800 B.C. Celtic invasion of the Islands.

By then, Nephilim giants had already explored the North American coastline, the Saint Laurence River and the Great Lakes, aware of copper deposits in the Great Lake region. To this day, the remnants of their mine still stands on a Great Lake island. No housing or graves are found at the site, so copper mining proved a seasonal, once-a-year adventure made by the hardiest Giants and any hardy Little People who worked for them underground in the mines.

Visit GreaterAncestors.com – link:

https://greaterancestors.com/great-copper-mines-of-michigan/

This site by Chris L Lesley is a gold mine!

And so, once the Celtic hoards swarmed the western islands - coming in from Spain and France - many of the British Giant/

Little People decided to move their clans west across the ocean into the empty but familiar lands of the Ohio.

How do we know this?

The henges of Ohio and the skull remains found inside of the Ohio henges generally match the henge designs and the remains of the Beaker era people of Britain and Ireland.

Once in America the two races continue to work symbiotically, but the Little People set up their own territory further south against the Smoky Mountains of Tennessee, with mountainous terrain their preferred natural environment for housing the families. But still, every spring, as in the days of seafaring copper mining, young Little People travel north to work the mines and the henges that they still build for sun worship, but now also purpose as burial tombs for the Nephilim Giant chiefs.

And so it was, for 2,000 years, from 800 B.C. until A.D. 1,200, as only in A.D. 1,200 did the Mongolian tribes from the west come across the Mississippi. Many, many tribes arrived, none of whom wrote, with all of their history regarding the Ohio Giants verbally passed generation to generation.

Verbal history is fragile. Furthermore, by A.D. 1,900, the tribes themselves begin to melt away into the modern era, and so, even oral history dried up. Only the notated A.D. 1,800 exchanges between European settlers and older Indians remain to tell the story.

They report the Giants white people with red and sometimes yellow hair, many around 6-foot, but the noble families, even the woman, standing 7-to-9 feet in height. For generations, the Giants held their own against the incoming Iroquois-Mongolian tribes, but A.D. 1,700 Indian folk law says that the Ohio Giants were finally exterminated "some 300 years prior", around A.D. 1,400.

It was then that the Cherokees slipped in south of the Iroquois, forging an alliance with the now abandoned Little People.

So what did the English American settlers think of all of this?

> *The eyes of that species of extinct Giants, whose bones fill the mounds of America, have gazed on Niagara, as ours do now.*
> **—Abraham Lincoln**

Back in Lincoln's time of 1838, as the English stock of America pushed into the wilderness, they routinely found skeletons of buried giants, 7-to-9 feet in height, usually found in burial mounds. It was common knowledge that another race had dominated America before the more recent Mongolian-American tribes moved in, tribes such as the Iroquois, etc.

Most of the skeletal relics found inside the mounds were reported by local newspapers (articles still intact), faithfully sent by locals to the Smithsonian Institute in Washington D.C. But by 1900, the thousands of skeletal remains sent to Washington all "disappeared", and thereafter, the Smithsonian denied their existence altogether.

This about-face regarding America's history came from the top of the U.S. government. As a policy statement, in 1889, John Wesley Powell, the head of the Bureau of Ethnology at the Smithsonian Institute in Washington, D.C., pronounced:

> *"Artifacts found prior to Christopher Columbus's arrival, would be considered illegitimate by the Smithsonian. Only the savage Indian culture would be observed."*

Since then, as the modern generations came and went, the very idea of giants faded from the American mind, and in more recent years even the mention of giants causes a backlash of ridicule by the scientific community. The "giant thing," in America, was successfully shuttered—no remaining evidence, no remaining memories.

Yet hundreds of A.D. 1,800's newspaper accounts survive.

Legend has it that at the end, the Iroquois encircled the last Giants on Sand Island, beneath the Ohio river falls, exterminating the nine-foot chief and all of his clan. The American Nephilim were no more.

However, their "Michigan copper" from the Great Lake mines—having singular impurities—does show up in archeological relics found world-wide. The copper survives, and yet the Ohio Giants are never mentioned.

Why are all of these back story examples ignored by modern academics?

CHAPTER 16

*Collusion — History Suppressed,
Primate Control Over Narratives*

This is an example of "forced ignorance" mentioned in SUBJUGATED's introduction.

Below we unravel the purpose of this "deception via omission," but first, a look at the old and new testaments of the bible, themselves byproducts of institutional agendas.

We already covered The Book of Enoch earlier. Besides this work, other works such as the Book of Jasher and the Book of Jubilees were specifically excluded from the old testament. Who knows what else came and went over the thousand years between King David and the time of Christ?

Besides Jasher and Jubilees — which are the more well-known works — other lesser ancient Hebrew *titles* are also mentioned in the bible, yet their content sits aside from the official Old Testament version. Works such as the *Book of the Wars of the Lord* (Numbers 21:14), the *Book of Samuel the Seer*, the *Book of Nathan the Prophet*, and the *Book of Gad the Seer* (1 Chronicles 29:29). Also, the *Acts of Rehoboam* and the *Chronicles of the Kings of Judah* (1 Kings 14:29). We also know that Solomon composed more than a thousand songs (1 Kings 4:32), yet only two are preserved in the book of Psalms (72 and 127).

In the New Testament, bishops attending the Council of Nicaea in AD 325 debated various written works about Jesus Christ and decided what to officially include within the New Testament. Much was left out, including writings of Jesus as a "hot-tempered" boy—making him appear too human. Since Nicaea, the Christian narrative has coasted along without disruption, reinforced by Christian intellectuals such as Saint Augustus in A.D. 400, and Saint Thomas Aquinas in A.D. 1.200.

Overall, with both the Old and New Testaments, great efforts were made to clean the narratives up, to steer them away from mankind- oriented storytelling to deity-oriented sagas. Things like Aliens, Nephilim, and Giants are scarce, mainly found in the ancient scripts of unfiltered writers, such as the Sumerians and Chinese.

These censoring operations should not come as a surprise. A premise of SUBJUGATED finds that ever since our creation in 4,000 BC, a tug-of-war has waged between primate socialist forces intent on controlling the Homo Sapient troop using any means possible including spinning reality, and the opposing alien libertarian forces who try to dig deeper into actual reality to optimize their wellbeing and their independent way of life. Most Alien-sourced Libertarians want nothing to do with institutions, and so, for the most part, primate-sourced Socialists fill the religious, scientific, medical, and government ranks.

These institutional types can't help themselves and need to keep everyone in the dark as much as possible to maintain discipline within the pyramid, a "need to know" operation controlled by elites.

Today, in this most recent era of Primate Socialist intent, while pursuing their agenda to subjugate Alien Libertarians, these institutional specialists have infiltrated all pockets of America's operating institutions, including:

Large Corporations, like Google and Facebook,
Universities, professors and administrators,
The Judiciary, prosecutors and judges,
The Medical Schools, FDA, Pharmaceuticals,
Government's unelected Deep State agents,
Show Business, writers, actors, and moguls, and
News Media's endless minions.

Socialist working inside the system to enforce obedience is a main tenant of Saul Alinsky's *Rules for Radicles* program.

> *Any revolutionary change must be proceeded by an attitude toward change amongst the mass of our people. They must feel so frustrated, so defeated, so lost, so futureless in the prevailing system that they are willing to let go of the past and change the future. To bring on this reformation requires the organizer work inside the system.* **—Saul Alinsky**

Today, mainly Primate Socialists hold the insider operational posts. Alien Libertarians are left to run privately controlled companies, big and small, including mom-and-pop concerns, the trades, plumbers, electricians, truckers, with many common-citizen Libertarians simply employees trying to stay strong.

This mosaic of narrative control underway since the beginning has been perfected just in the last 20 years, allowing the socialist narrative to echo through the corridors of all chambers of the civilization.

This is not conspiracy theory; this is how things are.

Entire books can be written on systemic suppression of history, but for now, I invite the reader to access videos on Ancient Giants that catalogue the global findings of this lost Nephilim race. By the way, the American Giants found in the mounds, lasted until AD 1,200 or 1,300, just recently. And don't forget the 75,000 Little

People graves found in Tennessee! Also, for good measure, read the lost books of the old bible, and the discarded works from Nicaea.

Now, let's turn the page, and learn a thing or two from Plato. In *Plato*, we dig into the nature of the genetic implant which elevated primate humans into Homo Sapient humans. It is not what you imagine.

CHAPTER 17

Plato & the World of Ideas

"I know this world is ruled by infinite intelligence."
—**Thomas Edison**

Plato's famous *allegory of the caves* teaches that we constantly misinterpret what we experience, that our circumstances often result from something of which we lack awareness or don't understand, such as solar eclipses witnessed in primitive times.

Using an allegorical storytelling form, Plato has cave dwellers sitting, facing a wall, their backs to a fire, with puppeteers projecting shadows onto said wall. The cave dwellers assume the shadows a final reality, neither realizing physical objects cast the shadows nor that puppeteers direct the movements of the masquerade.

Plato's allegory goes on to describe how enthusiastically the cave dwellers weave explanations around misunderstood experiences, coming up with all kinds of elucidations for the shadows, and how they stick to any cockeyed reason once it sounds good enough. Apparently, Plato concluded that self-deception resides prominently within the human condition.

And so, the reader should wonder about the three themes of this book: *Creation, Evolution and Intervention*. Which aspects of each are real and which parts shadow?

Overall, misinterpretation slows humanity down, leaving us saddled with inaccurate operating models, such as assuming the world flat because it *looks* flat. But occasionally we overcome shortsightedness, such as when Copernicus envisioned planets revolving around the sun, challenging the "Earth-centric" way things appear in the sky.

Over time, this ability to gradually uncover deeper realities has built up our many faculties including—get ready—mathematics, physics, chemistry, biology, geology, music, painting, sculpture, dance, cloth design, photography, theater, radio, film, sports, architecture, engineering, aerospace, toolmaking, energy harnessing, agriculture, animal husbandry, cuisine, weapon making and warfare, medicine, psychology and drug making, building, vehicle and communication equipment-making, not to mention philosophy, ethics, morality, theology, politics, law, finance, business administration, history, anthropology, and writing itself, et al.

Yup, we cover the lot, and no original primate Humans from the past demonstrated *any* sign of these possibilities. More so, no Earthly species extrapolated beyond what stood immediately in front of them, and hence no species ever developed a faculty for *anything!* Except Homo Sapiens. This ability to accumulate know-how is our true evolutionary track.

Most notably, the pre-Homo Sapient primate Humans and the Neanderthals lacked this knack for discovery. For hundreds of thousands of years they drifted, discovering nothing to lift them above their hunter/gatherer ways. Controlling fire—their claim to fame— was not a discovery; it was good fortune, and regardless, it did not matriculate simple Humans beyond the aforementioned stone tools, pottery, a simple vocabulary, cave art, and having a few domesticated camp dogs. On Earth, only Homo Sapiens constantly accumulated "know-how," a flow of progress referred to as a *teleological progression*.

What and why is this?

The reader might simply assume that Aliens caused a genetic boost of our IQs, and that this newfound intelligence explains humankind's ongoing story. But IQ just projects the shadow on the wall, a mere tool, and not the heart of our propensity to discover. Something more profound sits right behind it... but *what*?

Plato advocated a world of ideas sitting out there that we tap into. For example, we did not invent the *circle, the triangle,* or the *square*. These have sat within the world of ideas forever. The world of "forms," as Plato put it, exists somewhere, very much like an internet cloud database, but spiritually, not physically.

The universal recognition of circles, triangles, and squares presents an *a priori* (again, self-evident) proof that the world of ideas exists, a database, an "ontological encyclopedia of real and imagined beings." Certainly, all of these abstractions are not stored in our local *tabula rasa* genes, any more than the content of the whole internet resides on our smartphones. The smartphone fetches stuff from "above." We operate the same in connecting to "God's" mind. And I recommend the reader get religious about this!

In ancient times, we could not begin to realize the implications of the universe, its physical and spiritual dimensions, and thus the entry of Jesus Christ, the Buddha, and Mohammad, trying their best to use revelation to discover what lay beyond.

The world of ideas travels far beyond the housing of shapes. As with the humble circle, everything recognized (discovered) by Homo Sapiens during the past 6,000 years already sat waiting for us within the world of ideas. We just tapped in, and reciprocally, revelations occurred—as one must *try* in order to get a response! Homo Sapiens invented nothing on their own, including $E=MC^2$.

"Hey!" you might complain, "What about unicorns? Didn't we make these up in our heads?"

No! We made up nothing. Everything that we *recognize* was revealed.

Sorry to burst your bubble...

Atheist evolutionists hate this explanation. Evolutionists want neither God nor Aliens in the picture. They maintain that Humankind alone dragged itself from the jungle to where we stand today, and we did it our way, operating as loyal socialist primates, evolving slowly through mutations.

But contrary to evolutionary doctrine, a combination of Divine knowledge made accessible by Alien "tap-in" telepathy brought us here. Besides a few specific lessons taught to us by Aliens—such as the wheel, and how to make bricks—our interventionist Aliens gave us something much more important, a genetic implant that connects us to the mysterious world of ideas. Biologically this amounts to an organic transceiver in our neurons, an antenna of sorts. I'll expound by using a personal reference.

I am a songwriter, something for which I pined my entire life, and achieved late, in my 50's. The breakthrough came when I "opened the idea channel."

The idea channel feels a bit like revelation, as it occurs in a mild trance. The fresh idea (music in my case) arrives as an initial inspiration, followed by bite-sized information bits. You must remain open, fiddle with the incoming sounds and lyrics, and *yearn* for more bits so that you can *assemble* the whole thing. It's an elevated but uncomfortable, tedious state of mind and one needs deep motivation to stay at it.

Most artists operate like this, as do physicists such as Einstein. Albert claimed he would disappear into one of his thought escapades where a fuzzy understanding of something slowly became more apparent until finally, he could assemble it whole. $E=MC^2$, for example, stands as an assembled representation of his vision. My songs came to life as the assembled representations of what I was shown.

Sometimes it takes many sessions to collect the entire set of components required for final assembly. Bruce Springsteen says some of his songs hung around forever before he finally completed them. Once, *Rolling Stone* magazine asked Bob Dylan if "...he had written any new songs lately..." and Bob, well, expressed his dismay at the ignorance of the question, the reporter oblivious of the whole process. According to Bob, "No one writes a song unless they have to." It's that uncomfortable.

Michelangelo would let a block of marble sit in his studio for months until he finally saw the trapped "form" within. Then he would chisel away to discover the details, the "figure."

A songwriter might receive a song's chorus first, and the verses later. Or might get a guitar lick first that totally inspires, with more musical elements eventually entering as the so-called "composer" sits for hours playing the piano or guitar, contemplating the sound. The great ones such as Mozart brought in vast quantities of musical "suggestions" in order to assemble orchestral extravaganzas. Mozart would hear all of the instrumental elements in his head and transcribe these onto sheet music, all prior to an amazed Viennese ensemble bringing the entire piece to life.

In my case, I can handle country, rock, and blues songs, but Mozart's IQ surely dwarfed mine, allowing him to assemble musical architecture of much greater scale then my simple tunes. The process is the same, but the "dudes" involved certainly differ.

For me, at least, I find the trance state very uncomfortable, something I would not put myself through, except for the deep *yearning* I have to get the entire inspiration *assembled*, just so I can familiarize myself with it. Once complete, I have little recollection of any songwriting moments, and I sincerely tell people I did not write the song, I merely assembled it. When inventors or artists no longer *hunger to discover and assemble*, they stop producing wonderful works, their glory days over.

But everyone has some ability to tap in. Everyone has "light bulb" moments. The difference comes in how much *hunger-to-understand motivation* the person holds, and how much *assembly expertise* they have to then assemble what "it" reveals.

I, for example, know music theory. I play keyboards, trumpet, and guitar and have studied American songwriting from the 1800's on. I have worked within bands for 50 years, and have made hundreds of recordings, and so, when a new musical structure hits my antenna, I recognize its nature, and know what to do with it.

Einstein worked years in the patent office understanding new discoveries, and his brother-in-law was a first-class mathematician who converted concepts into equations, so they, too, finely practiced and honed their craft, not unlike like a musical team such as Lennon & McCartney.

The good news for Homo Sapiens: with such an abundance of the above-mentioned faculties available in which to become proficient, plenty of space exists for anyone *willing to apply themselves.*

The ability to *tap into the world of ideas* has two tiers. First, everyone uses the world of ideas to quickly understand what others have figured out. Certainly, most of us grasped the idea of smartphones right away, though we did not invent them ourselves.

Second, everyone yearns for the world of ideas once they badly need a solution, as in "necessity is the mother of invention." Some solely enter that pressure cooker when circumstances dictate, while others *voluntarily* enter this uncomfortable state to uncover new works... think Van Gogh.

But the larger point to all this follows: none of this *tapping in* occurred with the "standard-edition" Humans, the pure primate Humans who wandered out of Africa 70,000 years ago. They just kept on wandering until Alien genetic intervention enabled all the above. *Tapping in* is a specific genetic trait no species on earth previously possessed, way bigger than an odd mutation that causes something mundane, such as the rare appearance of an albino.

Once we got going with our new telepathic gift, impressive growth spurts and noted downturns in humankind's so-called teleological progression occurred. For instance, not much progress occurred during the Dark Ages. But the "discovery boat" took float once again, and as our base of know-how accumulated, the discovery process led to industrial, transportation, energy, and communication technologies, which in turn brought more and more people into the discovery game. What used to happen with the very few began to touch many. For example, in the 1950's, a few thousand books were published each year. Now, just in the United States alone, 600,000 books come out yearly, mostly self-published. Everyone wants their say the way once only available to Darwin, Poe, Twain, Dickens, and the Bronte Sisters. Microsoft Word transformed Humankind, as once had Guttenberg's printing press.

And so, to lump Homo Sapiens and human hunter/gatherers together within the same species shows an embarrassing lack of understanding of who we are. But to defend this genetic equivalency with no evidence of it whatsoever requires one to close a blind eye to almost everything. Why would people of science obstinately maintain that we are the same as the pure primate humans who left Africa 70,000 years ago? We will soon see.

But for the moment, if you will hypothetically accept that Homo Sapiens exists as a different species with different genes, do you still wonder about the Aliens and the likelihood of their role in why and how Homo Sapiens split from the human hunter/gatherers? Again, let's start from my personal reference point...

You may find interesting my second admission—that of my very own UFO encounter—more interesting than my first (that I'm a songwriter). Well, let's hope...

At age 13, I had just moved to Connecticut. One night, my cousins and I decided to spend the night in sleeping bags behind my parents' house. Chatting while gazing up at the night sky, we kids saw two luminous orbs rapidly approaching us. They did not slow, but suddenly halted 75 feet north of us, hovering a few feet above the tree line. They appeared about a foot-and-a-half in diameter. Both floated for mere seconds, when Orb #1 took off on a 90-degree angle west. Orb #2 stayed put for another few seconds, then descended directly south towards us. I ducked into my sleeping bag, remembering nothing else until dawn. Likewise, my cousin Gail remembers everything up to but nothing beyond the approach of Orb #2. So, I guess, put us down for a "Close Encounter of the First Kind." Anti-alien types attribute it to "ball lightning," but never explain how this ball of energy knew when to stop... and how to focus on us.

Although I don't argue in support of Alien intervention based upon this telling encounter, it certainly keeps me from scoffing at the idea. The reasons laid out throughout this book drive the assertion: Alien intervention remains the most likely explanation accounting for both our sudden rise on Earth and the unearthly behavior we have shown ever since.

Again, Homo Sapiens do not live within nature. We kill our own.

We lie. We deceive. We destroy. We dismiss.

We clearly lay claim to the worst invasive species ever, worse than poison ivy, something—even with our more noble qualities vouched for here—that neither God nor evolution would ever foist upon a global biosphere seeking Gaia-like (self-balancing) harmony.

We remain the only species whose intelligence timeline matures *after* its reproductive timeline. Dog intelligence stands near complete within months, and Fido does not reproduce until much later. Human timelines thus appear strikingly unnatural.

Consider also the fact that natural species possess an elegant uniformity to their appearance (so, for example, all zebras look great), whereas humans all look, well, *different*. Because, for the most part, we humans do not live up to an ideal, whether that's "Barbie," "Ken," or whomever. The rare genetic specimens, e.g., the George Clooney's and the Angelina Jolie's, look, well, *marvelous*. How could the one-in-a-million editions enjoying good looks occur due to natural-selection situation if every Monarch Butterfly displays perfection?

So, let's assume destabilizing intervention exists, but... so what? The answer—coming up next in SUBJUGATED Volume II – "History Re-imagined"

But first a few examples of Humankind's great inventors using revelation:

> "When I am traveling in a carriage,
> or walking after a good meal, or during the night
> when I cannot sleep; it is on such occasions
> that ideas flow best and most abundantly."
> —Wolfgang Amadeus Mozart

> "I think and think for months and years.
> Ninety-nine times, the conclusion is false.
> The hundredth time I am right."
> —Albert Einstein

JOHN LENNON

The *Beatle* song, "Strawberry Fields", written by John Lennon, has two components that fit well within this *Plato* chapter. The first aspect shows John's telepathy into the world of ideas, the second aspect considers the song lyrics themselves.

To start, when on a vacation break in Spain from The Beatles, John took a bus from Madrid to visit the medieval city of Toledo. While drifting off to sleep on the bus, the melody and lyrics to *Strawberry Fields* came to him. Having no tape recorder, John struggled to keep the song's image intact in his mind until he returned to the Madrid hotel to sort it out. Finally, with guitar in hand, he reverse-engineers the chords that underpin the melody. The combination of intricate chord movements juxtaposed against the exotic vocal melody line appears beyond human possibilities. The whole structure was simply revealed from above and assembled by John.

Second, the lyrics themselves reflect the mentioned concept of Plato's cave allegory as follows: "Living is easy with eyes closed, misunderstanding all you see."

Aye Johnny, the angels be talk'n ta you that day!

RICHIE HAVENS AT WOODSTOCK

Richie Havens was the first performer at Woodstock in 1969. All revved up, pounding his acoustic guitar—breaking strings—after performing for three hours, with a fresh guitar in hand, from the back of the stage he saunters towards the microphones until one finally hears the torrent of sound pouring out from him. Then Richie begins to sing:

Freedom, Freedom, Freedom, Freedom
Freedom, Freedom, Freedom, Freedom
Sometimes I feel like a motherless child
Sometimes I feel like a motherless child
Sometimes I feel like a motherless child
A long way from my home, yeah

Sing

Freedom, Freedom, Freedom, Freedom
Freedom, Freedom, Freedom, Freedom
Sometimes I feel like I'm almost gone
Sometimes I feel like I'm almost gone
Sometimes I feel like I'm almost gone, yeah

A long, long, long way from my home, yeah
Clap your hands, Clap your hands
Clap your hands, Clap your hands
Clap your hands, Clap your hands
Clap your hands, yeah, Clap your hands

Hey, hey, hey, hey
Hey, yeah yeah yeah yeah
Hey, yeah, yeah, yeah
Hey, yeah yeah yeah yeah

I got a telephone in my bosom
And I can call him up from heart
I got a telephone in my bosom
And I can call him up from heart
When I need my brother / (Brother)
Brother / (Brother)
When I need my father / (Father)
Father, hey / (Father)
Mother / (Mother)
Mother, hey / (Mother)

Sister / (Sister)
Yeah / (Yeah)
When I need my brother / (Brother)
Brother, hey / (Brother)
Mother / (Father)
Mother / (Mother)
Mother / (Mother)

Hey, yeah, yeah, yeah
Yeah-yeah, yeah yeah
Hey, yeah, yeah, yeah
Hey, yeah, yeah, yeah
Hey, yeah, yeah, yeah
Hey, yeah, yeah, yeah

The whole song came to him in real-time while on stage, pure telepathy and revelation.

Richie: "I think the word 'freedom' came out of my mouth because I saw it in front of me. I saw the freedom that we were looking for. And every person was sharing it, and so that word came out."

Notice as well, the revealed line: *I got a telephone in my bosom and I can call him up from heart.* This is the transceiver in our neuron system. For Richie, it was on fire that day.

STEVE JOBS

The ability for people to tap into ideas uncovered by others is explained nicely here by Steve Jobs:

Japan's very interesting. Some people think it copies things. I don't think that anymore. I think what they do is reinvent things. They will get something that's already been invented and study it until they thoroughly understand it. In some cases, they understand it better than the original inventor.

Finally, another explanation of discovery by Einstein:

The intellect has little to do with the road to discovery. There comes a leap in consciousness, call it intuition or what you will, and the solution comes to you, and you don't know how or why.
—**Albert Einstein.**

Plato was on the right track. Organic neuro-transceivers implanted into our gene bank 6,000 years ago explain how ideas are revealed and who we have become.

EPILOGUE

Hmm ...

"It is true that liberty is precious; so precious that it must be carefully rationed." —**Vladimir Lenin**

For those who have read this far I commend you.

You wonder.

For more, please read *Volume II – "History Re-imagined"*, a 5 Season, 35 Episode series that proposes the true drama of our Homo Sapient beginnings.

And please read *Volume III – "Genetics Drives Political Preference"* to see how our primate/alien genetics explain political conflict in the modern world.

"What are we to do with ourselves?"

www.ingramcontent.com/pod-product-compliance
Lightning Source LLC
Chambersburg PA
CBHW030325080526
44584CB00012B/716